CU00685433

Advance Praise for

The Little Book of Jeong

"In a year where human connection has been put to the test and physical interactions limited due to social distancing, Charlotte Cho's *The Little Book of Jeong* reminds us how important and powerful deep connections can be through Cho's career journey from Samsung in South Korea and as the founder of Soko Glam and Then I Met You. Most importantly: it's the call to action to slow down, be present, and revel in the deep appreciation for the people, places and things that hold a special place in your heart. Jeong is a universal concept that will change the way you see things and change the way you live—and it's the reminder we need today."

Karin Eldor, *Forbes* contributor and host
of the podcast *Share of Voice*

"*The Little Book of Jeong* is inspiring and generous in its wisdom. Charlotte Cho reveals the power of jeong in your life, guiding readers to find the most authentic, connected version of themselves. It's a book that will inspire you, empower you—a must read."

Catherine Cho, author of *Inferno*

"The entire work dissects the Korean notion of jeong by masterfully weaving in Charlotte's own personal anecdotes from her past and present. The result is an effective book that sheds light on why jeong is essential for living a well-rounded and connected life. Sweet, tender and oftentimes moving, Charlotte goes deep in her relationships and how they have shaped to become the founder she is today. A convincing case for why we all need jeong to have a more meaningful life."

David Yi, founder of *Very Good Light*
and author of *Pretty Boys*

"When writing about Korea, I often spend a lot of time contextualizing a definition of a word that doesn't have an equivalent in English, and Charlotte Cho has written an entire book about one of them that I have never even attempted to translate before! I loved her part personal memoir, part behind-the-scenes building-a-company memoir about her journey. *The Little Book of Jeong* is a tender-hearted deep-dive into the often inexplicable acts of love and the roots of relationships that take hold before one is even aware of it."

Frances Cha, author of
If I Had Your Face

The LITTLE

BOOK *of*

JEONG

The Korean Art of Building Deep Connections—
And How It Changed My Life

The LITTLE

BOOK *of*

JEONG

CHARLOTTE CHO

for Dave

My mentor, best friend, and ever-loving life partner.

Together, through jeong, we'll reach the stars.

Contents

Introduction

From the beginning, my journey of writing *The Little Book of Jeong* has been anything but conventional.

Three years after cofounding Soko Glam, I released my first book, *The Little Book of Skin Care*, which became an international best seller. Translated into ten different languages, it sold more copies than my agent and publisher had ever imagined it could. Ask any successful first-time author, and they'll tell you the next step is to write another hit. "Why don't you write another skin care book?" I remember my agent asked me. "Considering how many people enjoyed your first, it's guaranteed to be a success."

I said no. Between the book, Soko Glam, and The Klog (an online skin care resource guide we launched in 2012), I felt that I had enough channels to help people on their skin care journeys. It was through these outlets that I would be able to continue educating communities in real time.

There was another element of Korean culture, though, that I did want to share in my second book. It had nothing to do with skin care, but I was equally passionate about introducing it to the world.

That concept is called *jeong*. It's an important aspect of Korean culture defined as the deep and meaningful connections built between people, places, and things. It takes time to create jeong, but the process encourages generosity, empathy, and the cultivation of lasting bonds. Jeong is something that I learned about and experienced while living in Korea, and I believe it has profoundly grounded me in my personal life and led to the success I've achieved in my professional life.

When I tried to put this book out in the world, however, I was surprised to find that no one was interested. All of the publishers that had bid aggressively for *The Little Book of Skin Care* declined. My proposal was passed up several times; more than once I was asked to simply write a second skin care book.

So I decided to do what I've always done my entire life: Stay authentic to my passions—and find a way to build it myself.

When I started Soko Glam in 2012 with my best friend and husband, Dave, no one in America really knew what Korean beauty was and most people weren't thinking of buying skin care products online, especially from brands they'd never heard of. That didn't stop us. Neither did the fact that we weren't experts in e-commerce and didn't have traditional beauty backgrounds. I believed in what I was doing and now, eight years later, I'm proud to say that K-beauty is a global mainstay and has made fundamental shifts in the cosmetic industry.

I feel the same way now that I did back then. It's why I decided to self-fund this project and assembled a talented team of editors, illustrators, and designers who believed in my vision. What has resulted is not only a book about jeong, but a true expression of my love for Korean culture and the gratitude I have for the relationships I have built in this serendipitous life. All in all, it has felt invigorating to create something from scratch once again and to have the creative and editorial control to ensure my stories reach you in the way that I believe is best, which is true to me and my journey.

Why Read a Book About Jeong?

Jeong (also written as jung) is a Korean word and cultural concept that has no direct English translation, and to top it off, it can be tricky to pronounce. So why read a book about it?

Much of the world today is marked by superficial relationships, overwhelming anxiety, and a decline in empathy. I hope that learning about jeong will provide clarity about what's most valuable in life—in my view, that would be building deep and meaningful connections with the people who matter to you. Through my personal stories, I'll show how I came to understand the power of jeong and how it changed my life for the better. From giving me the chance to pursue my entrepreneurial dreams, to building strong bonds with my life partner, to strengthening familial ties and friendships and cultivating new relationships, I'll share how jeong has directly contributed to my happiness and success.

Throughout this book, I'll also emphasize the importance of practicing jeong through what I call *Simple Acts of Jeong*, which are practical ways that you can start to create these deep bonds. These are easy tips based on the pillars of jeong that I believe will open doors to a profound fulfillment that you might never have thought possible. After all, jeong is a feeling that is universal and that anyone can have. In fact, you likely already have jeong with others, but this book will teach you how to recognize it and let it blossom in your life. Lastly, if you're interested (or even obsessed) with Korean culture as I am, you'll gain a deeper understanding of how jeong is ingrained in Korean people and their lifestyles, from the way they eat meals to the way they nourish their personal and professional relationships. (Bonus: For K-drama obsessives, there are plenty of references to catch and enjoy.)

The Little Book of Jeong comes at a time when it's truly needed. In a world inundated with social media interactions (that make us, all in all, less social, ironically) and when we've forgotten (or grown lazy) about forging deep relationships, I believe that after reading this book and learning its principles, you will see for yourself how the power of jeong can transform your life.

If my stories can inspire even one person to build meaningful connections—and I believe that they can—then I'll know all the hard work was worth it.

Chapter 1

My Journey to Jeong

MY FIRST BRUSH WITH JEONG TOOK PLACE MORE than 10 years ago. It was a warm day in late November when I, only 21, arrived at my hotel in Houston, Texas. It was my first time leaving my home state of California alone, and I had been expecting bare-bones accommodations since it was a no-name spot near the airport that catered to business travelers. But when I swung open the door I found, to my surprise, the most luxurious hotel room I'd ever seen.

I was used to traveling lean, without any of the frills. When I was growing up, my family and I would drive from Los Angeles to Las Vegas and stay at one of those dirt-cheap $60-a-night hotels like Circus Circus. When I had traveled to New York the year before, I had crashed on the floor of a friend's apartment with nothing but a thin blanket. In college, I slept on a mattress on the floor, and for one summer, I even slept under my friend's dining table in exchange for cooking and cleaning their apartment.

So to me, this room was pure luxury. In fact, it wasn't even a room—it was definitely a suite. It had an entire living room and an enormous bathroom with sparkling white granite tiles. The towels were plush and fluffy like they had just come out of the dryer. There was a huge mahogany desk, where I plopped down my backpack. I sat on the soft queen-sized bed and stared at everything around me, wondering if the hotel had put me there by mistake.

Everything felt so surreal: Only two months after seeing an ad for an open position at Samsung in the *Korea JoongAng Daily*, an English daily newspaper, I had received an email from the company about my application. Getting a response was a surprise on its own. It was only partly written in English, and I had trouble reading the rest of it, which was in Korean. After finally deciphering it, I figured out that Samsung wanted me to come to Houston for an interview the following week and that they would put me up in a hotel and pay for my round-trip flight. As someone who didn't have a lot of work experience, I was a bit stunned. My family and my friends were also skeptical that I could ever land a job at one of the largest and most prestigious companies in the world.

But I was dying to get to Korea. I had become deeply

interested in the culture and wanted to learn the language. Despite the fact that my parents had both been raised in Seoul, I had never visited growing up and felt I had a lot to catch up on. I was fresh out of college and depressed over the prospect of spending the rest of my 20s in the same state I had lived all my life. With no responsibilities tying me down in California and up for a new adventure, I jumped at the chance to go to Korea. Within a few hours, I had my fingers crossed and a flight booked to Houston.

My interview was set to take place the morning after I arrived, and as the novelty of the suite began to fade, I started to panic. I realized I was utterly, hopelessly unprepared. I wondered if I would have to speak Korean. Why didn't I listen more attentively during those Saturday Korean language classes I took growing up? Better yet, why did my parents not speak Korean to me more regularly? I had friends who were fairly fluent, even though they had grown up in Southern California like I had; their parents and grandparents had made it a point to only speak to them in Korean. I was so nervous about what I was going to say and how I was going to sound in my interview that, even with the fluffy bed, I barely slept at all that night.

The next morning, I got up and got dressed. The only thing I felt prepared for was my interview outfit. To help me, I had watched a few Korean dramas that were playing at the time—*All In* and *Full House*—to get some clues as to what Korean fashion was like. I took some inspiration from Song Hye-Kyo, who played the lead in both dramas, and I opted for a mid-length black skirt with pantyhose and heels. Other than for a school play, I had never ever worn tights and was even confused about where to buy them (the mall or the grocery store?), but I did own a pair of black Steve Madden pumps and a white button-down. As I took a quick glance at my reflection in the full-length mirror by the hotel door, I felt a little more at ease. At least I *looked* suited for the position—though in hindsight, I probably looked more like a card dealer at a casino, much like the one Song Hye-Kyo played in *All In*.

Downstairs in the lobby, my heels click-clacked across the floor as I followed the Samsung signs to the conference room where the interviews would be taking place. I was greeted by a friendly and chatty Korean man named Woo-Shik, who looked just a smidge older than me. He started to speak in Korean, but I must have looked like a deer caught in headlights because he immediately switched to

English. "Are you here for the interview? For Samsung?" he asked. I nodded enthusiastically.

He led me to where I was supposed to wait with the other candidates and made small talk as we walked. "Hey, you live in L.A. right? Have you ever seen Nicole Kidman? What? No? How about Brad Pitt? Angelina Jolie?"

He started to rattle off names of celebrities like he'd just memorized the latest issue of *Us Weekly*. I tried to answer as honestly as possible—without disappointing him, of course—but the whole time I kept thinking, who is this character? Although he was smartly dressed, it didn't feel like the start to a professional interview at one of the largest companies in the world. But I told him about how I did once see Barry Pepper from *Saving Private Ryan* at a grocery store and started to relax. Maybe the interview wouldn't be so bad after all.

When it was time, Woo-Shik (who turned out to be the Samsung international recruiting officer) ushered me into a room with a chair in the middle. There were three older gentlemen, only slightly younger than my dad, staring back at me. They did not look like they were going to speak English. My shoes were starting to pinch. Oh my God, I thought to myself, I'm not prepared for this.

"Charlotte . . . Lee?"

"Yes."

"Thank you for coming."

"Thank you for having me?"

"한국말할수있어요?" (Do you know how to speak Korean?)

"조금 . . . 요." (A little.) I pinched my fingers together to sign language my Korean.

"미국에서 태어났어요?" (Were you born in the U.S.?)

Crickets.

"I was born in California. I'm sorry I don't speak Korean that well."

"It's okay. Samsung is a global company. If you work for Samsung, everyone speaks English."

A wave of relief washed over me as we switched to English, and they asked me about graduating from the University of California, Irvine and working at an ad agency. "It says here you graduated in 2006," one of them said, reading off my résumé, "but you started in 2003."

"Yes," I said, nodding. "I graduated in three years. It wasn't an accelerated program, I just took more units per semester and graduated early."

They looked at each other and started whispering to

one another. I tried, but failed to read the expressions on their faces. "Why would you want to graduate earlier?" one asked.

I swallowed and told them the truth. "It was cheaper," I said. "I paid for college myself, and three years was more economical than four."

More murmuring, looks, and nods.

"What do your parents do, Charlotte?"

I hesitated. I wasn't sure if sharing my dad's occupation was going to increase or decrease my chances of getting this job, but as soon as I caught myself hesitating, I felt guilty, as though I was ashamed of my parents. "My dad . . . he owns a store," I said. "A liquor store in Whittier." Then, maybe because of the guilt, everything else came pouring out. I told them how my parents *could have* paid for me to go to college, and in fact, they had wanted to so that I could completely focus on school. But I didn't want them to—they worked really hard, and they had already paid for enough. Besides, I'd had a job since I was 16. I liked being financially independent, and I saw no need to stop.

Telling these strangers about my parents made my eyes prick with tears, and I blinked them back as quickly as I could for fear they'd well up and spill over. Do not cry during a job interview, I told myself. You're going to look weak.

If they noticed my tears, the men didn't acknowledge them. Instead, they told me that they were sure my parents appreciated that; I nodded in agreement. There was one VP, sitting right in the middle of the group, who hadn't said a word the entire interview. He had a kind face, like a soft, fuzzy peach. Now, he spoke up, surprising me with the fluidity of his English. "Charlotte, how do you feel about public relations or communications?" he asked. "I think you'd be great for that team." I told him yes, I was interested in public relations. "And don't worry about the language," he added. "Samsung is a global company, and everyone is asked to speak English. You'll fit right in."

I smiled and thanked him, while my brain was doing backflips. What had he just said? What did he mean I'd be great for that team? Did I get the job? It couldn't be. They had hardly asked me any questions.

I stumbled out of the room in a daze and unsure what to feel other than relief that it was over. Back in the lobby, Woo-Shik asked me how much I had paid for my flight. I told him $486. He rolled out an envelope and handed me $500. In cash. And I was done.

Later that evening, my dad called and asked me how everything had gone. I tried to sum it up for him the best that I could: They had asked a few questions about my family, it hadn't felt like a real interview, and I hadn't thought I had done well, to be honest. But at the same time, I couldn't help but feel that I had the job.

My dad made it clear that he was happy for me either way. "That's great, Charlotte," he said. "Now get home safe." Little did we know that what I had just experienced in that room would change my life forever.

*   *   *

Within a few months, I found myself back at LAX airport, clutching a one-way ticket to Seoul after getting an offer from Samsung. Everything still felt surreal. I didn't know what to expect, so I started to set low expectations for everyone, just in case I failed miserably working in Korea. I told my friends and family that this would be a one-year thing and that I'd be back. I even told my brother he could borrow the new car that I had poured all my savings into (I had bought it prematurely, not knowing I would receive this unique opportunity) and to take care of it, so that it would be as good as new when I returned. One year would go by in a flash, I thought to myself.

I wasn't the most prepared for the move. I decided not to find an apartment in advance and luckily was able to crash with Jo, a friend that was living in Korea at the time. In my excitement over becoming a bona fide Seoulite, I bought a long black coat with faux fur trim that looked like it belonged in a Korean drama. I was moving in early March, which meant it would still be cold, especially for someone coming from L.A.

I was still confused about what I was going to do, but I practiced my Korean diligently in those weeks leading up to my departure. Still, I knew that one month of study wouldn't make up for 21 years of neglect. I reassured myself that everyone would speak English at work because that's what the nice VP with the pleasant smile had said. Regardless, it would be an adventure in a country I was excited about, so I was ready to wing it.

I remember my first day at work like it was yesterday. I was reunited briefly with Woo-Shik, who brought me to the floor where the Public Relations and Investor Relations teams sat. He introduced me to a burly man with a large humidifier that practically took up half of his desk.

I would eventually know him to be my direct manager, and he literally laughed at me and said in Korean, "I hope you know that no one speaks English in this team except for you." (Later, I would find out that many of my team members were so shy about speaking English that they had been dreading my arrival. Ouch.)

The day passed and I sat at my desk, tidying up for the twelfth time and looking at an empty email inbox. The next day, I was asked to physically cut a few relevant news articles about the industry out of the *Wall Street Journal*, paste them onto printer paper with a glue stick, then scan them into a file. The rest of the week I did the same thing, growing more and more defeated by the hour. I had been so excited to dive into a new career and work on impactful PR projects. Instead, I felt my ambitions were quickly dashed, and I was stuck with busywork that resembled third grade–level arts and crafts. To be fair, it's not like there wasn't work to be done, but I don't think anyone knew what to do with a Korean-American girl that only spoke English.

The next week was more eventful, but not in a good way. The whole team went out to lunch to welcome me. I ate my kimchi *jjigae* (stew) in silence until Mr. Hong, who was the head VP of my department, asked me to stand up and introduce myself. Not expecting this, I was mortified. Everyone stared at me as they waited. I slowly stood up, bowed awkwardly, then quickly stated my name and that I was happy to be there. If there were tumbleweeds in the city of Seoul, it would have been the perfect time for them to roll past. After my speech abruptly ended, there was scattered applause. As I plopped down into my seat, I wished the chair would disappear into a hole until it was time for me to go back to California.

Despite that being the most uncomfortable lunch of my life, my team didn't allow me to crawl into that hole. Every day from then on, I spent the majority of my time with the same people. Not only did we work together, we ate breakfast, lunches, and dinners together. Dinners at Korean BBQ restaurants were particularly special, as we huddled around the embers of hot coals, pouring drinks and cutting up only the tender pieces of meat for each other. Over our many meals together, they got to know the details of my family, my food tastes (and that I really could handle my soju, a Korean alcoholic beverage) while I got to quiz them on everything from politics to societal pressures in Korea. I even made friends with team members from different departments that were on the same floor, and we would grab coffees, take breaks, and plan out weekend activities together.

During stressful late nights at the office, we would take trips to the convenience store to fill ourselves up with snacks and cups of Maxim, my favorite Korean instant coffee. The dark, nearly silent floor was punctuated by sporadic fits of laughter as they taught me how to swear in Korean and poked fun at me by impersonating my terrible American accent. Day in and day out, throughout the bitter winter (the coat with faux fur did not cut it), I got to nourish these relationships and soon, I felt more at home. We got so comfortable with each other that they even made fun of my unbrushed hair and how little I knew about skin care—and I didn't mind. They were practically like my long-lost brothers and sisters.

Finally, spring came, which then turned into summer. It felt like I had just begun to settle into my apartment and was getting my multi-step skin care routine down pat when the trees started to change into fall colors. It had been my first time experiencing real seasons, and even I, who had predicted how fast a year in Seoul would go by, was caught off guard that my one-year anniversary in Korea was quickly approaching.

* * *

For the holidays, I made plans to visit my family in California, which meant I would be leaving for a few weeks. As I was saying my goodbyes, my colleague Sang-Ho, who was part of the broadcasting team, said to me in Korean, "It'll be weird without you here. I mean, we have jeong with you now."

"You have what with me now?" I asked. "Jeong? What's that?" My Korean had improved, but it was clearly one of many words that I still didn't know.

He tried to explain it. "Jeong . . . it's hard to explain. It's a type of feeling." He was struggling to find a definition, so he recruited Hae-Mi, another team member, to help me understand what he was talking about.

"Hey, Hae-Mi, what's the English word for jeong?"

She furrowed her brows and tried spitting out some words, but was ultimately at a loss. My other colleague Chang-Dong, who sat in the cubicle next to me, pulled up the dictionary on Naver. "Naver says it means affection."

Sang-Ho replied, "Hm, that's not it either. That's really a watered-down version of what jeong is."

Hae-Mi agreed. "Yeah, it's not exactly it," she said. "It's

much more complex than that. But when you feel jeong, you'll know it."

With that vague description, I wasn't sure what they were talking about. But curiosity got the best of me. I started to ask everyone around me, and the more it was explained, the more I grew to understand. I learned that jeong is a Korean word used to describe a deep and meaningful connection that builds over time and through shared experiences with other people, places, or things. I hadn't realized it at the time, but jeong had been present in my life from when I first landed in Korea. It was the countless dinners with the communal bottle of soju that we passed and poured gingerly with two hands into cups for one another. It was every late night at the office when a team member would take the extra time to help me translate the documents I couldn't do quickly myself. It was the feeling I got when my uncle woke up extra early, so he could drop me off at work when it was snowing the hardest. It was the 20,000 Korean won (about $20 U.S.) that was handed to me by my colleague so that I could get home safely in a cab. And I would soon come to realize that jeong had seeped into my every pore. I didn't just love my adopted city—I had jeong with Seoul and the people in it too.

Discovering jeong was when everything clicked. And the more I tried to understand it and cultivate it in my life, the more happiness and success followed. I thought often about the interview I had back in Texas. I hadn't been the strongest contender for the role, considering my lack of experience and inability to speak Korean. I wondered if my sudden display of emotion, filled with jeong for my parents, had played any part in their decision to give me a chance at this unique opportunity.

After a few years at Samsung, I ended up working briefly for that very kind VP who had interviewed me on that fateful day in Houston. Because the question still lingered, I worked up the nerve to ask him why he'd been so sure to select me for the position when I wasn't the most qualified candidate out there. He paused intently, as if it would be difficult to explain. Then he finally said, "I could see it in your eyes that you would have the same deep connection to this job as you do for your family."

And that is the power of jeong.

Chapter 2

What Is Jeong—And How Can It Change Your Life?

WHEN I THINK ABOUT WHAT I LOVE MOST ABOUT Korea, a few things come to mind. There are velvety sheet masks, drenched in my favorite fermented skin care ingredients. There's the excitement of sharing Korean BBQ, sitting around sizzling meat over hot coals with a green bottle of soju being passed around. There's the buzz you get from watching Korean entertainment— the electric dance moves of BTS or the never-ending feels of Korean dramas. There are the super aesthetic cafes that dot all my favorite neighborhoods. And then, there's jeong.

Jeong isn't something you can buy. It's a cultural concept that influences every aspect of Korean life, from your relationships with your family and friends to your career. Jeong is a complicated term; as my colleagues explained, it can't be easily translated into English.

Still, I've found that the following principles of jeong, when broken down, help make the intangible concept a little easier to grasp.

What is jeong?

Jeong: When you feel it, you know.

As I said earlier, jeong is one of Korea's most defining cultural concepts. Although jeong is better felt than put into words, the best way to describe it is a deep connection and emotional bond that builds over time and through shared experiences with other people, places, or things.

Jeong is omnipresent in Korean culture.

Jeong is so deeply ingrained in Korean society that it is constantly alluded to in everyday conversations. It's safe to say that every Korean person knows what jeong means, although they may struggle to describe it. If you're into Korean entertainment, you'll often hear it being referenced in movies, dramas, reality shows, and songs.

Jeong takes time.

Jeong doesn't come from grabbing a quick coffee with someone or sending a series of texts, no matter how witty the exchanges may be. It develops with time and requires your energy and investment to build over the years. To have jeong demands vulnerability and to experience both private hardships and celebratory moments together.

Jeong creates lasting bonds.

If you have jeong with someone, chances are you'll be willing to stick by their side and bend over backward for them, even when it may not make sense.

Jeong encourages generosity.

When you do bend over backward, you'll do it without expecting anything in return. While outside observers might find your generosity to be excessive or unreasonable, it makes perfect sense in your eyes since it was all in the name of your deep connection.

Jeong lasts forever.

Once you have jeong, you will always have that bond. You may not see that person or place for decades, but when you do, it will feel like no time has passed at all. Even when jeong turns to hate—like a falling out with one of your best friends—there will still be an invisible cord that ties you together, built from the many memories you've shared.

Jeong is different from love.

Some say jeong is like love. There are a few similarities, but jeong is a different connection than love because it's not romantic. You can have jeong with a group of friends from the neighborhood that you grew up in or a mentor that took care of you at your first job. Another thing that makes jeong special is the fact that it can be shared between larger groups of people—very different from the typical significant-other relationship.

And unlike love, there is no such thing as unrequited jeong. It's a feeling that is 100 percent mutual between all parties. Once you have jeong with someone, you never lose it. It's an unending connection that is never severed.

Jeong goes beyond the relationships you have with people.

You can have jeong with an object or any place that is deeply personal and meaningful to you. After spending five years exploring all that Korea had to offer, I had so much jeong with the country that it actually fueled my passion to start Soko Glam.

Jeong is good for the community— when used right.

Jeong is such a prominent part of Korean culture that people who are capable of having jeong are openly sought after by companies in the hiring process. To say someone lacks jeong is considered an insult, especially in social circles. Many people in Korea credit it for creating tight-knit communities that are stable and reliable because of how jeong motivates people to do good for one another without expecting anything in return. For instance, a young man helping an older woman cross the street safely with all her belongings, or a woman who makes warm home-cooked meals for all the neighborhood kids as if they were her own. These are both examples of how simple acts of jeong can foster a form of collectivism, which has become increasingly important among today's fragmented communities.

Jeong makes us human.

Jeong humanizes us because it inspires us to do more than what we have been asked to do—or what makes sense to do. Often, it comes hand in hand with empathy, or the idea that by connecting to someone's life experience, you might be compelled to help them in ways you would not otherwise. Some say that in order to have jeong, you must also experience *han*, which is the Korean word for a deep sorrow that is shared among all Korean people (I'll dive into the concept in a later chapter). Whether you experience *han* or not, the point is that empathy will help you fully understand others and establish deeper connections.

Jeong is universal.

Jeong is incredibly important to Korean culture, but it shouldn't be considered a uniquely Korean experience. It is truly applicable to everyone and present everywhere, across diverse cultures. Chances are you have already felt it and taken part in simple acts of jeong with those around you, but never knew its name until now.

Ultimately, jeong is best understood by living it— which is one reason why I decided to share my personal story through this book. Through experience, it becomes simple: When you feel it, you know.

How it changed my life.

After I learned how to describe jeong, I realized that I had been cultivating it unknowingly for years while growing up in California. Most of you will also easily relate jeong to the deep connection you have with family members like your siblings, parents, or grandparents. It makes sense that jeong builds quickly within a family unit due to the sheer amount of time you spend together: Living in the same house, sharing the same stash of toilet paper, arguing over the family Netflix account, you organically share so much of what life throws at you.

This was true of my relationship with my grandmother,

who raised me until I was in elementary school. She was in her 70s, a longtime widow (my grandfather passed away from cancer when my dad was only in high school) who chose to live alone in a tidy, one-bedroom high-rise apartment near Western and Wilshire with other seniors. Despite the fact that Koreatown in L.A. is the largest Korean community outside of Korea, I always worried about how she spent her time and how she got around. Her English was pretty scant, though she had miraculously passed her citizenship test by diligently memorizing all the questions and answers, leaving her fully prepared for every verbal interaction with her immigration officer.

"I'm fine, thank you . . . and you?" she would gleefully say to me, careful to overly enunciate each word and pause for effect, the way she had rehearsed many times over. It was her favorite English phrase because those were the magic words she believed had unlocked the gates to citizenship. My grandma was a firecracker with so much spunk and passion, but also a hot temper that often caused year-long rifts with her three sons. (Let's just say their wives—my mom included—didn't exactly get along with her either.) Despite having contentious relationships with her own sons, she and I got along very well—so much so that it was a running joke that I was the only member of the family she liked.

Even though she was a firecracker, inevitably age started to slow her down. She began losing her ability to move about freely. First she relied on a walker and then eventually needed a wheelchair to keep her mobile. As soon as I could drive, I made it a point to go to L.A. and visit her whenever I could, even though there was only so much we could chat about with the language barrier. To fill some of the time, and because she wasn't exactly free to move around, I wanted to ensure she had some form of entertainment—*The Tonight Show with Jay Leno* wasn't going to cut it. Luckily, there were plenty of Korean immigrant–owned video stores around her apartment. Those tiny hole-in-the-wall shops were important touchstones for the Korean-American community. Nowadays, you can easily stream Korean talk shows and dramas online, but back then, physical video tapes recorded in Korea were the only option. Those tapes were slivers of proof that their native land existed.

It took me just a short walk and a few dollars to rent a whole collection of Korean dramas, talk shows, and other programs that would be to my grandma's liking. Unlike the nearby Blockbuster with its Hollywood new releases spaced evenly on shelves, these video shops made use of every inch of wall. There were tapes lined from floor to ceiling, rows and rows of black VHS with plain white stickers that had the recorded show titles written in Korean. Sometimes I wouldn't be able to get my hands on a hot K-drama series for weeks. If I was lucky to land my picks, I'd leave with a black plastic bag overflowing with tapes, already rewound and ready to pop in the VCR once I got to my grandma's place. Then, after a few seconds of flickering as the picture settled into frame, we'd finally start to binge (yes, even on VHS!).

Thinking back on the many hours I spent at her apartment, we didn't really have to say much: We just rolled the tapes. And off-screen, I found so much to observe. I got to see the corners of her lips turn up when the two lovers serendipitously ran into each other, their affection shown through an innocent grazing of hands (or even pinkies). I got to see, from the corner of my eye, her tears flowing at the end of a particularly emotional scene, as I tried to blink my own away. Whenever the ending was terrible, she made it known with snide remarks. I didn't ask many questions, but I got to know a little more about her through these small moments we shared. I also grew curious about the life she had left behind in Korea. Even as I acknowledged the cheesy sheen of Korean dramas, I couldn't help but become invested in their real-world setting. They gave me a glimpse into the highly charismatic side of Korea that I had shunned for so long.

Yes, it may be hard to believe, but until that point, I had possessed zero interest in the country of Korea or being Korean—period. My older sister, Michelle, was fully on board the K-train, plastering H.O.T. posters on her wall and obsessing over the "fact" that Kang-ta had looked directly at her while she stood in a sea of thousands of screaming fans at Wilshire Theater. Meanwhile, I was on the opposite end of the spectrum. I grew up ashamed of being Korean. I had no role models in American mainstream media and no real connection to the culture, other than the terrible Saturday Korean language classes that I absolutely dreaded. Some kids in my neighborhood had bullied me for having "slits for eyes," which I internalized. Part of me likely wanted to rebel against what my older sister liked, too.

Although the tapes were meant to appease my grandma, I quickly became the one enraptured by the magic I saw on screen. Those dramas changed the lens through which I viewed my heritage, shifting toward a more positive light. Watching them together with my grandma, splayed out comfortably on her apartment floor with a plate of honey-dew she had cut into perfect little squares, only made the warm feelings grow stronger. Whatever subconscious negativity I had felt about being Korean began to slowly melt away. I didn't realize it at the time, but those hours we spent in front of the TV were overflowing with jeong. There was the jeong I built with my grandmother, which drove me to want to know more about her and dive more deeply into our shared roots. From there, my intrinsic curiosity and desire to learn about life in Korea began to build, leading me to the world of Korean dramas, to the *JoongAng Daily* where I saw the ad for Samsung, to my new life in Seoul. Those first seeds of jeong with my grandmother slowly but surely changed the course of my life.

When You're in the Mood for Jeong: Korean Dramas

There's something wildly addicting about K-dramas, and clearly I'm not alone. They've become a global phenomenon: You don't have to be Korean or understand the language to be a superfan, and even a streaming content powerhouse like Netflix is churning out drama after drama. I'm all for it— there is nothing, and I mean nothing, that gives me more feels than Korean dramas.

I believe that the secret sauce is *not* svelte actors with shiny, voluminous hair and perfect skin (though I admit that helps *a little*). It's the jeong that is depicted in each plotline and between characters that makes every episode so deliciously sentimental that it'll hook in anyone with a beating heart.

To me, mainstream Hollywood shows tend to be more formulaic and never spend enough time on the evolution of relationships. (I was a film and communications major, so I do feel somewhat qualified to make this hypothesis.) Their portrayals of these relationships often fall flat, as they generally prioritize sex scenes and special effects over the meaningful backstories that allow you to truly empathize with both protagonists and antagonists. Korean films and dramas, on the other hand, have a way of focusing on backstories and drawing out the evolution of jeong between the characters, portraying their personal struggles in the past and their convictions to succeed in the future. They're so well-crafted that often by the end of the first episode, I'm already weeping over a box of tissues, in a way that no Hollywood movie or series can compare.

Consider how many Korean dramas start off with the lead protagonists not getting along, even at times hating each other. But through serendipitous meetings and shared experiences, they eventually start developing a bond. When they finally realize and confess their love for one another (the ceremonial peck on the cheeks or lips), it is their beautiful development of love, *and* more importantly, jeong that makes me squeal with happiness. As for Korean films across genres, the characters' life experiences are always constructed to provoke a wide variety of emotions: They make me cry, laugh, have butterflies, *and* feel scared in one sitting.

I have to admit, Korean dramas have come a long way from when I enjoyed them with my grandma. The ones you might see on Netflix today are a bit more inventive and sometimes even a bit risqué with their plotlines (I think I choked a few times from the overt sexual innuendos in *It's Okay to Not Be Okay*). Today they tackle important topics like mental health, sexual harassment, and even racial inequality—which I welcome. But the essence of jeong remains in every scene as the core driving factor that makes people of all ages, races, and genders fall deep into the stories. If you're new to Korean dramas or Korean cinema, here are a few for you to try. (Make sure to look out for the many references to jeong; they call it out naturally because it's so ingrained in the culture.) I guarantee that when you feel it, you'll know.

My Top Jeong-y Korean Dramas

The *Reply* Series (*1997, 1994, 1988*): Witness the portrayal of intimate bonds between childhood friends and their family members and stir up your own feelings of nostalgia for your youth.

It's Okay to Not Be Okay: Beyond the appeal of the show's strong and empowering female lead, the plot shines a light on the importance of mental health through its depiction of an emotional journey toward healing.

My Mister: Not your typical romantic K-drama. Jeong develops between the protagonist and her boss as they bear the weight of life's hardships, which helps them both heal and overcome their individual challenges.

Itaewon Class: An ex-convict with strong values works hard to become a successful entrepreneur, and his mentality of giving without expecting anything in return is reciprocated by those who support him on his journey.

Start-Up: Struggling entrepreneurs are forced to make many important career and life choices as they reach for their dreams. The question is, will they make decisions based on their hearts or their heads?

My Top Jeong-y Korean Films

Train to Busan (Director Yeon Sang-Ho): Alongside all the heart-stopping scenes—e.g. hordes of zombies chasing after passengers on a KTX train— there are many instances of self-sacrifice and jeong as the characters struggle to survive.

Parasite (Director Bong Joon-Ho): The movie's timely examination of income inequality and greed may seem like the antithesis of jeong, but it's counterbalanced by the existence of deep bonds among the inner circles of each family.

Assassination (Director Choi Dong-Hoon): A deep jeong for Korea is on full display in this historical espionage film, which follows a tight-knit group of resistance fighters.

Okja (Director Bong Joon-Ho): This action-thriller shows us that jeong does not exist between humans alone. When Okja, a genetically modified super pig, is kidnapped, her human owner, Mija, embarks on a full-scale rescue mission, driven by the strength of their 10-year-bond.

Chapter 3

There's Nothing Like a Shared
Meal to Nourish Jeong

A S IT TURNED OUT, ALL THOSE KOREAN DRAMAS I watched with my grandma could not have possibly prepared me for what was to come—working in a real-life office at the largest conglomerate in Korea and adjusting to a completely foreign work culture. Within the first few weeks on the job at Samsung, I found out that I had missed the chance to join the company with a designated class of new recruits, who go through a month-long training session together. Samsung was famous for this elaborate program, which was held off-site at a dedicated campus in a remote spot a few hours drive from Seoul. The new hires learn all about the company's history and corporate values, but more importantly, they get to know each other on a highly personal level thanks to Samsung's enthusiastic approach to team-building. Think intense 5:00 a.m. hiking trips to see the sun rise together and shared plate after plate of *samgyupsal* (grilled pork belly), with lots of late-night conversations and drinks in between. When they come out of it 30 days later, they leave with life-long friendships that help them get through their time with the company. In other words, it is a jeong-building camp.

The closest American experience I can think of is moving into your college dorm for freshman year, completely away from parental supervision for the first time. For me, it was absolutely imperative that I entered the adult world by drinking 40s of beer in a parking lot and indulging in 1:00 a.m. ramen binges (plus the occasional streaking session) with my peers. (Yes, all true stories.) The result? A year of new experiences (both highs and lows) with a core group of friends embarking on the journey with me—friends who I still cherish and speak to regularly, even to this day.

Since I was a new recruit from the U.S., I was not part of Samsung's traditional class and instead was put through a condensed four-day training program. Most of the people I met in that session were going to other global Samsung offices in cities like Abu Dhabi and Houston, so I wasn't getting the benefit of a robust jeong-building camp that would help me ease into corporate life in Seoul. I never would have imagined wanting to go to a company training session, until I realized how crucial it was in Korea to have established bonds in the workplace. Without them,

I braced myself for the first few weeks as the new kid at a new job—in a new country!—stuck eating a sad lunch alone at my desk until I could find someone to join me.

But things at Samsung were done differently. At noon, the lights went dark on our office floor, oddly reminding me of the way nap time began in preschool. That was our signal to file downstairs to the cafeteria, where lunch was served Hometown Buffet–style. Everyone ate lunch in the cafeteria due to Samsung's collective work culture, and the cooks and kitchen staff had to run a tight ship to feed more than 1,000 people every day.

You lined up in front of a long table with plates and cutlery at the head and a row of silver buffet trays filled with so much delicious food. There were heaps of steaming white rice, spicy chicken doused in *gochujang* (red chili pepper paste), surrounded by potatoes and onions. There were stacks of *gim* (dried seaweed), and you could hear the clatter of chopsticks and spoons being passed around to the people still standing in line. At the end of the meal, you would drop off your tray by the exit and drink a cup of water (common Korean knowledge says that drinking after a meal is much better for digestion), then head upstairs for a quick nap at your desk (which was completely normal).

To my surprise, even after my awkward welcome lunch, I had someone to eat with every day—because as soon as the lights turned off, we as a team went downstairs and ate together, as did every other team. Everyone, no matter how busy they were, would drop everything they were doing to join their core group. And even if you were new or shy, you always had a team to eat with. Yes, you might make plans with a friend outside the office or have a more private lunch with a colleague. But on those rare occasions that I didn't join my team, they didn't let it go easily. "Is everything OK?" they would ask in Korean. "Did you eat?" (*Bap meogeosseo?*) some would say with a sincere look of concern (words that I now realize are deeply layered with care for your well-being).

I had no qualms about eating alone. There were plenty of times in college that I would walk around the UCI campus, gulping down a Double-Double from In-N-Out or a Vietnamese banh mi sandwich from Lee's, the only two affordable options nearby for students. Besides, it's not like you feel like striking up a conversation every day. And sometimes I would get self-conscious because my teeth are magnets for red chili pepper flakes. On days that they served spicy dishes (almost every day—who am

I kidding, it's Korea), I would have to hold a full conversation without moving my lips. Sometimes it was just easier to be alone.

But after a few months, I finally realized that the communal dining found in Korean culture has its perks because of the way it helps you create deep connections without even trying. People weren't picky about who they ate with, and they never considered it a chore. Instead, they always made sure that those around them were eating well. At Samsung, there was almost a sense of duty to spend every lunch and frequent dinners together, and many of us benefited from those opportunities to nourish jeong.

You'd start to learn about everyone's food likes and dislikes, about their children, and talk through their weekend plans. You'd figure out what kind of jokes they liked to tell, and what was on their mind when they looked worried. Through our conversations, I got a better understanding of what made my teammates tick and found out what they were really like, away from all the endless meetings, glue sticks, and PowerPoint presentations. Sometimes, if we wanted to chat a little more, we would go grab a quick latte once we'd finished eating. Others would walk around the building or take a group stroll to Yangjaecheon, a nearby stream, for some light exercise. There was something comforting about simply enjoying each other's presence, even without exchanging words. People worked so late in the office—until 8:00 p.m. or long after—that our lunch hour was taken very seriously. In fact, it was one of the only moments we were free to socialize. It could not go to waste.

Looking back, I'm sure my colleagues were not thrilled to spend their lunch hours with a Korean-American who couldn't joke the way they could. (I thought their jokes were hilarious, I just couldn't come up with a witty response in Korean.) It may have even stressed them out when the conversation became stilted, or they might have felt they were being judged by me, their pseudo-English tutor. Despite all that, they never let me eat alone. Studying and working in the U.S. was completely different. I remember at my first desk job, after college at a small advertising agency, I would either eat alone at my desk or walk to a fast-food joint next door, hunched over my tacos as I scarfed them down in silence. Though it was and still is socially acceptable to eat alone, I have to admit, it was pretty lonely.

Thinking back, my colleagues' persistence during each

precious lunch hour was what got me through the lonelier months of my time in Korea. I feel so thankful for that, even a decade later.

Simple Acts of Jeong

- *Don't eat at your desk every day*—grab a colleague and go out to lunch at least once a week. It might be awkward at first, but you'll be surprised by how quickly you can get to know each other outside of the office. If you're trying to save money, don't fret. Offer to eat a bagged lunch together at the park, or just grab a quick coffee in the afternoon.

- *Make regular plans* to spend time with your classmates, mentors, colleagues, friends, or family—any relationships that you want to build. They say face-to-face time (even digitally via FaceTime or Zoom) is the new luxury. It's harder than ever to get on someone's calendar. Make it a point once a week to meet someone new and someone you already know. After a year of regularly planning these meetings out in advance, I found that I had really nurtured my old and new friendships.

- *Don't flake.* Things happen, but after two or three cancellations, you start to gain a bad reputation. It becomes more and more difficult to earn that trust back. Think of each meeting like a promise to someone special. If you must cancel, remember to apologize sincerely and plan better next time so that it doesn't happen again.

- *Hard to find time for a relaxing lunch or coffee?* Why not run errands together? Go grocery shopping or to the gym. Even the most mundane activities can be fun when you have someone to do them with.

Why Korean Food Tastes (and Feels!) So Good

My love for Korean restaurants goes deep. It's more than the delicious BBQ and the colorful (healthy!) banchan (side dishes) that you wrap up delicately in a perilla leaf with soybean paste and roasted garlic. And it's more than the fun of watching dishes cook right in front of you, so that they're still piping hot when you devour them. And yes, although it is well-documented on Instagram that I love the green bottle, it's more than that refreshing sip of clear liquor that gets me excited. Actually, it has nothing at all to do with the amazing food—it's the way eating at a restaurant in Korea makes me feel.

During my time in Seoul, I didn't find jeong only by eating with others. There was a sense of warmth and familiarity that overcame me when I stepped inside every restaurant, even if it was a place I had never been to before. I spent my first year living alone in a small studio in Yeoksam close to the office. (When I say small, I mean less than 200 square feet.) I wasn't cooking much—my kitchen wasn't well-equipped, and I frankly didn't know how to make anything beyond eggs and ramen—so I relied on little neighborhood spots for *kimbap* (seaweed rice rolls) and *seolleongtang* (ox-bone soup). As I kept going back, the friendly owners of those mom-and-pop shops started to take me under their wing. They gave me extra helpings of side dishes and even engaged me in conversation, so I wouldn't spend all my meals there solo. They felt like my long-lost uncles and aunts whenever they asked me about my day and about my life. It was a scene I could only imagine taking place because of jeong, and that made me feel warm and fuzzy inside (not just from the ox-bone soup).

I felt less lonely just by dining out, and I was reminded with every meal why sharing food can nourish such warm bonds. Next time you go to an authentic Korean restaurant, look and listen closely for the following—you'll feel it too.

Your Server Feels Like Family

First off, when you're in a Korean restaurant, it's common to address the waitress by the Korean words *noona* or *unnie* (older sister, as addressed by men or women, respectively) or *emo* (auntie), depending on age. That being said, no matter how much older the woman looks and unless you're very young, I would not recommend calling the waitress *ajuma* (older woman)—*noona* or *unnie* will suffice and may even score you better service.

These are pretty intimate words that you would never dream of saying to your waiter in New York—unless you were OK with getting weird looks from them. Even I felt awkward using them at first because those words felt so personal. Growing up, I had barely even called Michelle, my own blood-related sister, *unnie*, so calling a stranger *emo* or *unnie* felt like crossing a line. But that's how it's done, and they often call you *unnie* right back. The words make you feel at home, as if you're sitting at the dinner table and your family is serving you like always.

Korean Honorifics Can Make You Feel More Warm and Fuzzy

You won't only hear the use of the word *unnie* in Korean restaurants. *Nopim-mal* (Korean honorifics) is a large part of Korean language and culture that plays a role in social structure and interpersonal relationships. The origins of this complex language system can be traced back to the country's strong history of Confucianism, which places a high value on hierarchy and respect for elders.

Here's how it works amongst friends: once you

become more acquainted with someone, it's common to address them with familial honorifics, whether you are related or not. For example, an older male friend earns the title *oppa* or *hyung* (older brother), while an older female friend becomes *unnie* or *noona* (older sister). (See the chart on the next page for more details.)

The moment you switch from a friend's full name to an honorific such as *oppa* or *unnie*, it acknowledges the deeper connection and brings on the fuzzy feelings, accelerating that journey to jeong. If you turn on a Korean drama or movie, oftentimes you can observe when the honorific titles come into play. Although I only speak in English to Dave, I do call him *oppa* from time to time (though he says it's only when I'm trying to sweet-talk him into doing something for me).

Of course, not all honorifics conjure up feelings of camaraderie. *Jondae-mal* (formal honorifics) are used to show respect for those who are more experienced or higher ranking than you. For example, the use of *nim* (used after a proper noun) is the highest form of honorifics: *Sajang-nim* (boss) is a formal title used for CEOs and *eomeo-nim* (mother) is used when addressing your mother-in-law. I grew to understand the importance of these titles while working at Samsung; it was a sign of respect to be referred to as *daeri-nim* (assistant manager) by my lower ranking colleagues, once I got promoted from the associate level.

Oppa (오빠) = Older brother (used by females)

Noona (누나) = Older sister (used by males)

Hyung (형) = Older brother (used by males)

Unnie (언니) = Older sister (used by females)

On the whole, I found it to be refreshing. The servers were not only fast and efficient, they went above and beyond by cutting up the meat on the grill without expecting any tips. It reminded me so much of family dinner: the exact same way that my parents would carefully cook and cut up the meat into bite-sized pieces, then place the juiciest morsel on my plate. That simple gesture evoked an indescribable feeling of warmth, no matter who did it.

When we sat down to eat, we would first reach for the cutlery and napkins, which were often kept in hidden drawers at the table. Setting up and serving each other became another part of this intimate dining experience. Instead of politely waiting for our waiter to check on our table, we would shout out "*yeogi-yo*!" (over here) or "*unnie*!" Imagine you are at your own house, you want your sister to bring more water to the table, and she is in the kitchen within earshot. Wouldn't you just yell at her from across the room? It's practical, it's easy, and it's family—so it's OK. And that's what it's like in a Korean restaurant.

Why Sharing Really Is Caring

In America, there were so many times that I would go to a restaurant, scan the menu, and order my own dish without consulting anyone else at the table. And if I regretted my choice, I would just silently drool over my friend's more appetizing plate while I sadly ate mine.

In Korea, no one ever asked if we could share—every meal was ordered family style. As soon as the food arrived, someone at our table would spring into action and start splitting little portions into everyone's bowls. It didn't matter if some of us were strangers, or if it was our first meal together. And among friends, if someone had ordered something like a soup or *bibimbap* (a rice dish with assorted vegetables and meat), which comes in a single bowl, we could slip our spoons in without asking. It was an unspoken rule that the dinner table was a free-for-all. When you're like family, it's not a big deal.

Sometimes, when the mood was right, we would even feed each other. Whether it was my teammate, my uncle, or a friend, they would wrap a piece of meat for me in fresh lettuce with garlic and kimchi, claiming it was the best bite yet and that they were making it just for me. I felt so much jeong when they presented it to me with two hands, or once we grew super chummy, popped it directly into my mouth! I would always happily accept it. I love food, and I can confirm that it tastes a million times better when you eat all together.

Simple Acts of Jeong

- *Express your gratitude.* I'm definitely not advising you to call your waiter "older sister" to foster jeong. Instead, simply look your waiter in the eye, address them by their name (if they have a name tag!), and say, "Thank you for my _____." It really does go a long way. Through these actions, you recognize them as people first and by the work that they do, rather than acting entitled to the service. As someone who's worked at a restaurant, I can tell you that you'd be surprised by how little guests acknowledge your presence or effort.

- *Host a potluck party.* These are so fun because they're a collective effort and a shared experience, where you get to try different dishes that people are proud of making. You may even pick up a new recipe or two.

- *Next time you're at a restaurant* with your friends, ask if they'd like to order family style. Some cuisines are easier to share than others—Spanish *tapas* are small shareable plates by design—but you can make it work with any food and enjoy more of what's on the menu.

- *When eating family style*, pass the food around before you serve yourself. Or, take it a step further and serve everyone directly. There's nothing classier than taking care of others first before you dive in.

- *Be present.* There's nothing worse than meeting someone who is glued to their phone. I myself struggle with this constantly—we're biologically engineered to seek the hit of dopamine that comes with every new email or text. Start dinner with your phone out of sight and keep it there. No matter how slyly you think you are glancing at your screen, it's extremely obvious to the other person. A shared meal is so much more special when you both give it your undivided attention.

- *Food doesn't always have to be shared.* If you know someone who is sick, grieving, or just in need of a pick-me-up, stop by and drop off something delicious, just so they know you're thinking of them. If they live too far from you or need their personal space—or you think it's a little too old-school—consider putting in a Grubhub or other delivery order that goes straight to them. It's a modern take on the neighborly casserole drop-off, and it just might make their day.

About the Bill

It's not uncommon to see a group of Koreans fighting for the check at a restaurant. I've personally seen a person yank the bill out of someone's hands and yell at the cashier to demand they accept their card over the other. Now I catch myself doing the same with other Korean-Americans and with my own family members. I've literally ripped a bill in half in an attempt to swipe it away from a friend.

Growing up as a Korean-American, long before I moved overseas, I was so perplexed by this sight. I couldn't understand it. Why would anyone fight for the bill? Wouldn't you want the other person to pay, if they were offering?

After immersing myself in Korean culture, however, I realized that it was a jeong-filled gesture. It's not all about proving your generosity. Fighting to pay the bill implies that there will be many shared meals in the future—that your companion can always grab the check next time. There is something playful about it too, when you're so close that you're demanding to treat each other. It shows the relationship is not tit for tat. No one is dividing the bill by cents like in the U.S., where people tend to go Dutch and everything is split evenly, sometimes even down to the last penny.

There is also a sense of hierarchy, duty, and chivalry that comes into play. When I first joined Samsung, I was confused by the fact that every single lunch and dinner was paid for by my boss or an older team member. After every meal, I would bow deeply, so thankful for their kindness. They would always laugh at my earnest behavior, while the other employees who were also being treated didn't bat an eye. I quickly learned that it was simply customary for the oldest person to cover the meal, as it was implied that at their age they had more means to provide, and it would be expected of me later in life. And as I rose up the ranks in age and title, I found myself reaching for the bill to pay it forward to my younger colleagues—no question about it.

Simple Acts of Jeong

- *Actions speak louder than words.* If you've invited someone, treat them if you have the means to do so. It sends the message that this is the first of many meals you'll share together, and maybe they'll make the effort to invite you the next time.

- *Resist the urge to always go Dutch.* Every meal doesn't have to end with a split check or a Venmo payment request. Trust me, your generosity and spontaneity will be remembered and will inspire them to be just as generous in the future.

The Ins and Outs of Korea's Crazy Drinking Culture

I could write a whole book about Korean drinking culture alone, which I consider second to none, but let's just say I'm glad I spent my early 20s in Seoul. It's the perfect place if you love to go out. So many bars stay open all night and into the morning, and you could get home cheaply by taxi even before ride-sharing services took off. Your average Korean loves to drink—*a lot*. (Fun fact: South Korea's hard liquor consumption rate is reportedly the highest in the world and more than twice that of Russia, which comes in second.) A bottle of soju can be bought for less than $2 at any convenience store, which makes it incredibly economical compared to the $20 cocktails I see here in New York. It's usually taken neat and tastes crisp, like a milder version of vodka.

I think of it like a panacea for all moods. When you're feeling sad, you bring out the soju. When you're feeling happy and celebratory, there is soju. Couples who drink it give into cheesy yet wonderful displays of affection (it's a trope in Korean dramas for a reason). It can be mixed with beer as *poktanju* (bomb shot), fruits, *makgeolli* (fermented rice wine), and Yakult, a probiotic yogurt drink. (Warning: Mixing soju with any of the above creates a risky combination.)

So much of Korean culture revolves around social drinking, but I want to talk about how it plays into *hweshik* (work dinners) that are paid by your boss. *Hweshik* can be large department-wide affairs or organized among smaller teams. Usually they're planned and marked by an event, like if the company has hit a milestone or if someone is joining or leaving the team. Sometimes they're set up for no reason at all—just a spontaneous excuse for good old-fashioned fun. When I was at Samsung, we would have a *hweshik* every other week; I heard other departments were going every other day.

Korean offices tend to foster a fast-paced and high-stress work environment, especially at major companies like Samsung. Naturally, drinking was a big part of these dinners, but there was more to it than just getting drunk to cut loose. In fact, there is a concrete set of drinking rules that applies in both social and professional settings. First, no glass should ever be left empty, but no one should pour their own drink. Everyone at the table keeps their eyes peeled for refills, and if someone were to go around and pour for every glass, you would grab the bottle from their hand before they got back to their own.

In most cases, especially if you are younger, you would use both hands to pour and both hands to receive by carefully lifting up your own glass as a sign of mutual respect. This two-handed pose is not limited to drinking, but applies in a wide range of situations: You use two hands to present and receive a business card, to exchange money between a cashier and customer, to take a bag at a shop after making a purchase, and to even pour and receive lotion samples at skin care stores. If you were drinking with a person of note, such as your boss, you might turn away to drink the shot as an additional sign of respect. But with close friends, you can top off and drink with one hand, no problem.

When I heard about these rules, I felt like I was learning a sacred ritual that really nurtured generosity and emotional connection. I especially loved how these drinking traditions, some of which date back to the 1300s, had persisted to this day, even among the younger generation. And no matter his age, I find something irresistibly charming about a man who holds the bottle with one hand and places the other near his chest as he pours (another version of the polite two-handed pose). That was one benefit of the *hweshik*: Just through this simple act of pouring for each other and sharing our favorite spirit, we practiced and developed so much mutual respect and trust.

One would think that after all those late nights at the office, no one would want to spend more time with their team at a long dinner, drinking into the night. Personally, I was fascinated by this *hweshik* culture, which was so unlike anything I'd experienced in the States, and I dutifully took part. I liked discovering new restaurants; as for the free food and drinks, I was more than happy to partake. It's true, however, that some of my teammates would complain about each pending *hweshik*. There was definitely a sense of obligation to attend these dinners, and for anyone who didn't like drinking, there would have been a lot of pressure to participate. I was fortunate to have a lot of women on my team—there was no pressure to "keep up with the boys," which I've heard can happen—and a boss who didn't blink twice at someone drinking only water. I'm sure other departments and other companies were different.

Nowadays, a lot of Korean companies have steered away from the traditional *hweshik* in favor of healthier alternatives that promote a better work-life balance. Teams might catch a movie together or go bowling instead. In many ways, that's a great thing. I know that too much drinking is not good for your health, and there are a lot of consequences to a wild night out. But it makes me kind of sad. I found something so special about eating and drinking the night away with my colleagues, and it took our friendships to a place of comfort and ease, in the way that you only really let loose with those that you trust. I have so many beautiful memories of those intimate dinners.

Over steaming bowls of soup, we would feed each other while being frank with our feelings and our frustrations. We'd hash out our issues with a frustrating manager or a new company policy, then wash down all those grievances with a shot or two. The next day, even if matters weren't clearly settled, the thoughts and feelings we were able to express helped alleviate some of the tension and stress.

After dinner, we usually went off to a *sool jip* (a type of bar) for more drinks and food. (Food is always part of the equation, so much so that food that is made to have with drinks has its own name, *anju*.) Then we almost always ended up at karaoke, which was considered our *sam-cha* (third round, as in our third stop of the night). We belted our hearts out and drank until 10:00 p.m.—sometimes till 1:00 a.m. The next day, we'd show up sheepishly to the office, a little (or a lot) hungover, and we'd grab yet another meal together like *haejang-guk* (soup to help ease your hangover). Sometimes we would find little bottles of Bacchus, a Korean energy drink, on our desks, a small but meaningful gift distributed by a team member who empathized with our pain.

When I worked at an advertising firm in California, we would go to dinner once a year for the holidays. Working in New York at Soko Glam, I would go to happy hour once in a while, but they were few and far in between and usually done with smaller groups. There are more boundaries and balance this way, which I completely understand and respect. *Hweshik* culture does take away from personal time. But throughout my journey with Soko Glam, I have often grown wistful, thinking about how at Samsung, many of my strongest friendships came through those shared nights.

It's one reason why I've tried to hold onto those traditions, in some small way. Every year at Samsung, our entire department would take a weekend trip, packing our bus with boxes and boxes of snacks and driving a few hours away from Seoul. We spent hours eating, drinking, playing games, and talking until 4:00 a.m., then hiking through the mountains at sunrise and getting to know each other better through inside jokes. Several years later when we went Soko Glamping, our own version of a jeong-building camp—a weekend in upstate New York, filled with just as much hiking, team-building exercises, and late night talks—I was happy to see that the bond-building effects were just as strong on either side of the world.

Whenever I fly to Seoul and meet up with my Korea-based Soko Glam team, though, I'm grateful that I can really relive the old days—especially since three of my former Samsung colleagues, Mr. Hong, Ji-Hyun, and Hye-Ji, now rank among them. They wait for my flight to touch down in the evening, and by 8:00 p.m., we are catching up over sizzling beef and gulps of soju—just enough to help me get through the jet lag.

Simple Acts of Jeong

- *Not interested in drinking or still underage?* Koreans love meeting up for a cup of coffee just as much as they do grabbing drinks. In fact, there are so many coffee shops in Seoul that one out of every seven buildings has one. (As of 2018, there were an estimated 66,231 coffee shops in South Korea, making Seoul's coffee-per-capita even greater than that of

Seattle or San Francisco.) Wherever you are in the world, take a friend out for coffee, tea, or a healthy juice. Regular one-on-one time is special, no matter what you're drinking.

Chapter 4

Good Jeong, Hateful Jeong

I HAD BEEN IN KOREA FOR ONE YEAR AND TWO MONTHS when I met Dave. We were set up by Sara, a good friend of my sister's from back home who knew Dave from high school. Since we were both expats in Seoul, Sara thought it might be a good match, so we agreed to a blind date. Well, not completely blind—I had spent the greater part of one evening stalking his Facebook profile, diligently scrolling through all the photos of parties he'd been to in the past year. He'd been to *a lot* and some girls may have been put off, but I thought he had cute puffy cheeks that I immediately wanted to pinch. By the time we had our first meeting, I had already memorized his smile.

"If you don't hit it off, don't worry," Sara had told me. "He has a ton of other friends living in Korea that you can meet through him." Excellent, I thought to myself. I welcomed this contingency plan, as I had already failed a series of *sogaeting* with the native boys.

Sogaeting is the term for a blind date set up by a mutual friend. I was surprised when I first heard about them since blind meet-ups were rare in the States at the time, well before the rise of dating apps. In Korea, though, it was the standard. All my single friends and coworkers would have a *sogaeting* lined up through the weekend; some of them told me they went on over 100 in a year! It was also common to keep an eye out for good prospects for your friends, particularly for those friends with whom you had jeong. Everyone was looking out for each other.

I realized early on that it wasn't common to meet or network with new people at places like bars, for example, because unlike in America, where chatting up strangers in public feels more natural, Korean culture at the time was focused on personal "introductions," both in business and love—hence the *sogaeting*. Intrigued, I started telling my native Korean friends to set me up. Before agreeing to go, you usually ask about the person's height, age, job, and sometimes for a photo, but you don't get much deeper than that. For a while, I simply enjoyed them as an entirely new experience I'd never have in the U.S.

The last *sogaeting* I went on was with a native Korean guy who was undeniably handsome, had perfectly styled hair, and was fluent in German, English, and Korean. He ghosted me after two dates. Later, our mutual friend who arranged the date told me that he didn't like how I had failed to use honorific Korean in my texts when we had just gotten to know each other, though I knew that was only an excuse. He knew I was terrible at Korean and unaccustomed to the proper use of honorific etiquette in dating culture. By the time Dave and I had set our first date, I was so discouraged by the cultural barrier with native Korean men that I was excited to meet someone with whom I could hopefully find a deeper connection.

We agreed to meet for a glass of wine after work one day in May. Beyond my Facebook research, the only things I knew about him had come from Sara—that he had gone to high school in Fullerton, California, graduated from West Point, and was working on an army base. When I saw Dave standing outside Artisée, a popular coffee and dessert chain in front of my office, I was pleasantly surprised. Never mind that his shoulders looked broader in person (extra points in my book), but we hit it off immediately. He told me he was a captain in the U.S. Army, stationed in Korea after a tour in Iraq. We wound up talking for four hours—until we were literally kicked out at closing time—and we realized how much we had in common, having both been raised in Southern California by hard-working immigrant parents from Korea.

Turns out we had grown up only a town away from each other. We both had microwaved plenty of Hot Pockets and babysat ourselves as young as age 8. We bonded over the fact that our parents could never afford a proper babysitter or daycare for us or our siblings. When he was young, he had been instructed by his parents to not pick up the phone and instead use the answering machine as a way to screen calls to ensure no one would realize he and his brother were unsupervised. I related to this deeply, as I had been at the Whittier Public Library with my sister Michelle just 12 miles away, wandering the stacks until our mom or dad picked us up at 9:00 p.m. when the local library (aka free day care) closed for the night.

Dave and I had both worked as soon as it was legal to do so. He was at a coffee shop in the Brea shopping complex, making lattes and chocolate fudge squares for all the soccer moms, and I was working as the cashier at an all-you-can-eat sushi buffet at the Puente Hills Mall. We bonded over these similar experiences, and it almost felt like we had known each other our entire lives. Although jeong doesn't happen overnight, things were definitely clicking between us. There is a Korean saying, "정들었다" (jeong duel-eottda) used to describe the feeling of jeong that has permeated between two people, and from our very first conversation, there was a part of me that felt we were already laying the groundwork for it.

The next day, I left for a quick weekend trip to Beijing, and as my plane was taking off, I closed my eyes wishing I was landing instead. I couldn't wait to get back.

A few days later, on the bus back home from the airport, he texted me, "Are you back?"

I responded, "I was just thinking of you." It felt a bit forward for people who had just met, but I knew what I wanted.

He would visit me on his lunch breaks in full army uniform: dark sunglasses and a beret that slyly covered part of his forehead. I loved that he wore tough-looking boots, but had a baby face and almond-shaped eyes that made him look so gentle and trustworthy. Before meeting Dave, I had no preference for a man in uniform, but suddenly it became incredibly charming. (That beret was everything.)

It might sound cheesy, but I truly felt like I was in a

Korean drama—dressed in my frilly blouse and pencil skirt, running through the turnstiles of our office as Dave waited for me in the lobby. Standing there in uniform, he was shrouded in mystery. My colleagues would whisper and look curiously at the man who would take me out once or twice a week. Being one of the few expats, it drew a lot of scrutiny that I would dare punctuate my work day with a lunch date in between. I didn't mind. All I needed was the chairman's son to fight for me in a dramatic love triangle to complete the story.

It's true what they say: It doesn't matter where you are, it matters who you're with. Together, Seoul was suddenly twice as much fun to explore. We spent hours drinking at a *pojang macha*, which are outdoor tented food stalls around the city, clustered with our friends over steaming pork belly and lettuce wraps, and afterward, with the smell of garlic and grilled meat still on us, we belted our hearts out in private karaoke rooms.

We loved to head out to cities like Busan and Damyang to find incredible hole-in-the-wall restaurants, and we never felt as in sync as when we would decide to splurge on *hanwoo* (Korea-raised cattle known for its marbling; one of the most rare and expensive types of beef). During late-night summer picnics along the Han River, we'd talk for hours, pouring out all our hopes for our careers, our families, and the future, but we also put all our worries and vulnerabilities out in the open too. It was the combination of moments like these, so raw and real, that built our deep bond with each other.

Looking back, we spent our 20s together in the best way. We were young, careless, and free, soaking up everything—both the good and the bad—that the dynamic city had to offer. Over the next four years, as we explored the nooks and crannies of Korea, we not only began to build a deep jeong for each other, but for the country too.

Finding Jeong With Korea

As I mentioned earlier, jeong is not something you have with people alone. You can have it with an object, like the suitcase you took on all your travels; a beloved pet, like I do with my dog, Rambo; or a place that you hold dear. For me, it became clear that I was starting to build jeong with more than my colleagues, my friends, and Dave. I began to have a deep connection with Korea too.

It was easy to have jeong with Korea because it was so

deeply ingrained in the culture. The ideological elements of Confucianism that had come from China and taken root in Korea centuries ago—the importance of loyalty and community over self, as well as the duty to give in relationships—had fostered the collective mindset that I felt everywhere.

Like a ripple effect, it made me pause and reflect in ways I hadn't before. Growing up in the U.S., I remembered the deep bows that we kids would perform in front of our parents every Lunar New Year. It felt like a superficial action—we did it dutifully, but only for the money we received in return. It wasn't until I learned about jeong and witnessed those bows once again in Korea that I realized the meaning behind them. It meant that elders were respected as a key part of the community. Children were taught from a young age to remember that and treat them well. I loved that.

What struck me the most, though, was the overwhelming jeong that Korean people had for their country. I'll never forget the 2010 World Cup. Seoul's Floating Islands, a cultural hub on the Han River, had just been built, and right next to it, the city had set up a massive outdoor screen to show the games taking place in South Africa. Dave and

I walked together from our houses in Seocho down to the river, joining the parade of people marching together in their "Be the Reds" shirts, which was the team's slogan. We screamed and cheered for the Reds, for Park Ji-Sung and his teammates Cha Du-ri and Lee Woon-Jae, as they successfully advanced to the knockout stage. It rained that day, but we didn't care! In our ponchos, sitting in a sea of red, we all screamed and cheered as one. With jeong comes unity and pride, and that passion for Korea was infectious—many of my non-Korean friends living in Seoul were also swept up by the excitement. It makes me smile just thinking about it.

A few months earlier, during the 2010 Winter Olympics, Kim Yuna, known as "the nation's daughter," had executed a triple lutz-triple toe loop combination, a triple, and a double axel for the short program, which not only won her the gold medal, it broke records. Stuck at the office, my colleagues and I had huddled around a small TV on the fourth floor, watching as Yuna performed her free skate program flawlessly. At that time, my jeong for Korea was still growing, but theirs was overflowing. Tears streamed down their faces, and they held their breaths in anticipation and awe, as every movement was executed to perfection. At the end, we could almost see the weight lift from her shoulders, the overwhelming sense of relief. As the first South Korean skater to medal at the Olympics—a gold medal!—Yuna's achievement, her dedication, and her sacrifices intensified the feelings of jeong around the country so that you could feel it radiating off of everyone's faces that week. I don't doubt that she felt it too—she would then go on to perform her free skate program "Homage to Korea," which was a rendition of the Korean traditional folk song "Arirang" in the 2011 World Championships. To me, this was just another example of jeong at work that ultimately resulted in her unshakeable dedication to her homeland.

I marveled at the fact that tiny Korea—only about 52 million people, compared to 329 million in the U.S.—had grown so fast, and in a matter of decades, had gone from extreme poverty to become the 12th largest economy in the world and a major player in so many industries—from TVs, cars, beauty, and electronics to the soft powers of music and entertainment. All that without any real natural resources to speak of. I had so much jeong with Korea that my heart also ached for my parents, who immigrated to America 40 years ago looking for better opportunities.

Like so many Korean immigrants I knew, they had never gone back to visit, choosing to leave that part of their lives behind. But Korea was no longer the third world country my parents remembered. In fact, many of the buildings in Gangnam below the Han River eclipsed anything I had seen as a kid in L.A.'s K-town, which honestly looked like it was stuck in the early 1990s.

A small part of me felt guilty. I knew my mom had never wanted to leave Korea and had never imagined the struggles she would face as an immigrant; she had to leave without finishing her college degree and had uprooted herself from her friends and family to a place where she couldn't speak the language. My dad had sacrificed a lot—a well-paying job as a college-educated manager at a respected manufacturing company—to open up a liquor store in Whittier, which meant a lot of hard physical labor and late nights in front of a register. Even though I knew many Koreans would still have envied them for the freedoms they had gained (the grass is *always* greener) and despite the fact that my parents had so much to be proud of (all that they had provided for our family), I often thought about how they could have been part of the transformation. A part of me didn't even want them to know what it was like living in modern-day Korea, in case they would regret having come to America in the first place.

Simple Acts of Jeong

- *Building jeong takes time and effort.* If you're new to a city and feeling lonely, you must get out there! Spend your weekends exploring all the nooks and crannies of your new area. Go deeper with the community, whether it's getting to know your barista at your local coffee shop or joining a community group, like a photography or hiking club. It's the people you connect with that will help build the emotional bond with your city.

Why Jeong Translates Into Passion

The next three years passed by in the blink of an eye. Dave and I were newly married and living happily in an apartment in Itaewon with Rambo. I was still working at Samsung and had been promoted to an assistant manager. Life had become a series of predictable routines. I felt comfortable and at ease at work, except for the occasional nagging feeling that I wasn't being challenged enough. Even socially, things had fallen into a pattern. We had our usual set of friends that we spent time with on the weekends, always starting at dinner and somehow always ending at *sa-cha* (round four—yes, it goes beyond three) at a karaoke room. This hard-working, hard-partying lifestyle seemed natural to Korea, and we took to it like fish to water.

As with any close relationship, my feelings toward Korea were often in flux. There was a natural ebb and flow between us, just like how couples squabble and make up again and again. I didn't always see Seoul through beautiful rose-colored glasses. Over the course of five years, there were a lot of days where I felt I never wanted to leave, but there were also days where I felt frustrated and questioned why I was staying so long.

One late night after work, a cab driver refused to take me home because I lived too close to the office. It's illegal to refuse a fare based on transit time, but it occurs often anyway, and the driver had grown aggressive when I tried to express myself with my stunted Korean, which was doubly frustrating. I came home to Dave in a sour mood and started ranting about how much I hated Seoul's traffic and how rude the driver had been. That sparked something in me, and all the little things that annoyed me so much started pouring out.

I hated the pervasive passive-aggression, like how we all had to stay late at work because our boss was still there, or the way that I was dismissed at times for being a young woman. Korean society seemed excessively concerned with self-image—there's a reason why plastic surgery rates were the highest in the world at the time—and it sometimes came into play professionally too. At a Samsung dinner with journalists, people would comment on our looks; even when it was complimentary, it always felt highly inappropriate.

In that same vein, I found that people cared far too much about their status and name recognition in every facet of their lives. I was always asked what college I had attended, what company I worked for—and if you had gone to an Ivy League or worked at a prestigious brand like Samsung, you were automatically revered. I thought it was crazy how much people spent on designer goods, but eventually, it started to affect me. (Or so I realized when I caved and bought a Chanel purse that I couldn't even afford.)

As a liberal American, I also struggled at times with the comparatively conservative culture. I didn't like the taboo nature of topics like the LGBTQ+ community; at the time, Koreans generally didn't acknowledge them or even shunned them, and many of them still do today. The sexism was rampant, as well. For example, at the time it was considered taboo for women to smoke, but it was completely acceptable for men. Sometimes, I would smoke at company dinners in front of my teammates just to make a point. I didn't really enjoy smoking at all, but I wanted to break that convention.

Yes, as much as I loved Korea, there was a great deal I disliked about it too. I told Dave I was ready to leave. After almost five years, I thought it might finally be time for me to return to the States.

Miweon Jeong

Wondering if you can possibly have jeong with a person, place, or thing that you dislike? It's called *miweon* jeong (affection based on negative feelings) and is the opposite of *goweon* jeong (affection based on positive feelings), aka the loving jeong I've described up until this point.

A simple way to understand it: Many long-time married couples have both *goweon* jeong and *miweon* jeong. Imagine that you're angry with your spouse, who has a bad habit of coming home late from work. But as the hours pass, you start to worry yourself sick. Once they finally arrive, you become angry again, although deep down inside, you're glad they made it safely—that's *miweon* jeong. It's human nature, and in the end, all jeong is rooted in passion.

In the heat of the moment, I hadn't noticed Dave was excitedly gripping a letter. I recognized the emblem and instantly knew it was something that he had worked so hard for: the notification of his early acceptance to Columbia Business School. While any respectable wife would have been ecstatic for him, I took one look at the packet he received and started bawling.

"Why are you crying? You just said you wanted to leave!" he said with a lot of concern and a little annoyance. But through my tears, I could tell by his expression that he had anticipated my reaction to the news. We had so much jeong between us that sometimes he knew me better than I knew myself.

I immediately wanted to take back everything negative I had just said about Korea. I was happy for him, but it suddenly (and selfishly) dawned on me that I would be leaving. I had more jeong with Korea than I could have ever imagined, and I realized how much I had taken for granted. I began to regret that I hadn't been able to explore nearly all the places I wanted to. I knew I would miss all the addictive TV shows that had me pulling all-nighters. (This was before streaming platforms—now, luckily we can all enjoy Korean shows worldwide!) I wouldn't be able to have *jjajjangmyun* (black bean noodles) delivered to my door. (This was pre-Uber Eats and Seamless.) New York subways would never be as clean as Seoul's, I bitterly thought to myself.

As hot tears spilled over my cheeks, I remember telling Dave that if we left, there would be nothing to bring us back. We didn't have close family to visit or any real reason to return. "I don't want to lose my connection to Korea," I said. I wished there was something I could do with my life to share what I loved about the country with the rest of the world.

At the time, I didn't realize how those feelings would change both our lives.

How the Power of Jeong Built Soko Glam

I have no doubt that my jeong with Korea is what gave me the actual courage to create Soko Glam with Dave, but it didn't start out as a business venture. We didn't set out to make tons of money, there was never a business plan with investor pitches and marketing objectives, nor did we ever dream of hiring departments or teams. It started with our simple wish to find something that would shine a light on what made Korea special to us and would keep us connected to the country and place we had so much jeong with, even when we moved back to the states. As Dave and I began tossing ideas back and forth in our Seoul apartment, grappling with the reality that we would be heading back to the States in a matter of months, I thought the best way to stay connected to Korea was to share a part of Korean culture that I was most passionate about.

That something was skin care. Seeing my skin transform through my own five-year K-beauty journey, I had become a firm believer in its power. But it wasn't just my newly glowing complexion that made me a fan. The entire Korean skin care philosophy gave me more confidence than I had ever had in my life. It was the self-care I needed with its daily and nightly rituals, and it also satisfied that bit of nerdy Charlotte that loved diving into the ingredient list and deciphering what worked for which specific skin types and concerns.

What I loved about the Korean beauty industry was the variety and innovation, which I thought was unparalleled—such unexpected ingredients and gentle, natural formulations. Everything was incredibly accessible in price, so there was something for everyone. But even more than that, I traced my passion back to the tips and recommendations I had excitedly exchanged with my colleagues and friends each week. Our shared obsession with skin care had made me feel truly connected to something for the first time.

Growing up in America as an Asian-American, awkwardly straddling two worlds, I had never quite fit the mold of what was conventionally beautiful. I didn't have any role models that looked like me, and I had always felt lost. When I saw magazines in Korea, where women had dewy skin—and it was always healthy, the most important standard in Korean beauty—and the same jet black hair and almond eyes as I did, I felt so much pride for my culture and like I finally belonged. I wanted to celebrate this type of beauty and share it with the world.

It was a light bulb moment for me and Dave when we decided to open up an online store in December of 2012— only two months after Dave received his acceptance letter—that would give people outside of Korea access to my favorite skin care products. I had already been a "curator" for my friends in the U.S., bringing back products for them on holidays, so I thought it would be easy to start doing it more officially outside my friend circle. On a blog,

I would share my tips on how anyone could build a multi-step routine and get to better skin days. I had a lot to share!

We decided to call it Soko Glam because I had always loved New York and dreamed of living in Soho, but I found myself in Seoul after college instead. So I used that to come up with the name: "Soko," a portmanteau of the words South Korea, and "Glam," because I always thought healthy skin was so glamorous and a confidence-booster that surpassed even makeup.

Back in 2012, Korean skin care was not mainstream, and skin care itself was not as top of mind. Beauty trends were hyper-focused on the color cosmetics and fragrance categories. And forget about customers shopping online, let alone on your phones. This was pre-Instagram influencers, and there weren't many independent skin care brands to choose from; people stuck to the usual legacy labels from L'Oréal and Estée Lauder. Naturally, everyone we spoke to told us Soko Glam was a terrible idea.

"Do you really think that people would want to shop for foreign skin care brands they've never heard of, online, where they can't touch and feel the products?" my friends asked us. Admittedly the odds of this working out were slim. Not only was Korean beauty relatively unknown in the U.S., but Dave and I didn't come from traditional beauty backgrounds and didn't know a single thing about e-commerce, let alone how to run a business. And in general, 90 percent of startups fail within the first year.

But all the naysayers and their skeptical comments rolled off us like water off a duck's back because we didn't really care. We didn't care if Soko Glam was just a side gig, or if it barely made us lunch money. The desire to work hard and do well was fueled by our jeong for Korea. Learning about these Korean beauty secrets had changed my life, and I knew I would find deep personal fulfillment in helping others navigate this world. All I wanted was to share some of that feeling with others, and I knew they would come to love it as much as I did.

Jeong Can Be the Rocket Fuel You Need

Starting something new—like a business idea or even a hobby—then putting it out there in the world for everyone to see is one of the most frightening things I think you can ever do. Especially in this social media age, where you can easily find out what that kid from your sophomore year gym class is up to 15 years later, it's especially tough to try something that you might fail at publicly.

Fortunately, there's a key that unlocks a lot of courage, and that's jeong, of course. For me, it was the jeong I had for Korea. For others, it might be for a son or daughter or another family member. I have heard many personal stories from entrepreneurs who began by addressing a problem that concerned those they cared deeply about, then became extremely successful.

There is something to be said for letting a deeper connection guide you, or having a mission that goes above and beyond your basic self-interests. It will help you stay the course and make better decisions for the big picture, no matter how long and challenging the journey may be. Some of the hardest and loneliest moments of entrepreneurship would make anyone want to quit, and no one can prepare you for creating a company from scratch—or the bumps in the road you will encounter as it scales. I know that if we had focused only on profit or fame, we wouldn't have made it through. You need to be rooted in something deeper and something more intrinsic to what you value. In my case, it was my passion and eagerness to stay connected to Korea. Knowing that I was making a bigger impact and contributing value to Korean beauty allowed me to stay the course.

I find that chasing the things that you think sound good on paper or are purely superficial—money, status, or fame—will only bring you so much happiness. I've met founders that were motivated just to make a quick buck and capitalize on a trend; they usually fizzled out if they weren't emotionally invested in the idea or passionate about its reason to exist. It's not only obvious to me: Customers are smart and can see through those intentions.

As Soko Glam grew, we began to offer things that most e-commerce experts did not recommend. We poured our resources into The Klog, a separate online resource guide to educate people about their skin. We offered complimentary consultations with our Skin Concierge to those who wanted to get started on their skin care journeys. And as the curator, I refused to sell products that were trendy on Instagram if they had suspicious ingredients or claims. It had to be effective and good for your skin; most of the time, the things that went viral simply weren't.

I felt a powerful sense of duty and a heavy weight on my shoulders. More than money or fame, I was motivated by my pride and love for Korea. I wanted to represent it well and share what I loved most about it with others, and I wanted to make sure that anyone who heard of K-beauty and shopped our curation would have a good experience and see actual results that would make them believe in Korea's skin-first philosophy. I wanted to stand up for my country. That and helping others experience the same transformative connection was far more important to me than making money off a viral mask.

This is what drives me and Dave, even to this day. Our jeong for Korea has helped us persevere, and it has even helped me gain the courage to pursue new projects outside of Soko Glam that would challenge me in different ways. In 2018, I launched Then I Met You, my own premium skin care line. I wanted to focus on using highly effective ingredients and crafting a sensorial experience, and because I was so passionate about the life-changing power of jeong, I decided to make it the ethos of the brand. Since jeong was a foreign word—and one without a simple English translation—no one could understand why I would want to fuse such a complex idea into a skin care line. Why not simply call it "Soko Glam" or name it after myself? But I chose the phrase "then I met you" to nod to the moment when someone or something enters your life and changes it for the better, which is something I associate strongly with jeong. I felt that jeong was a cultural concept that our communities would benefit from knowing, and I was encouraged to use Then I Met You as a way to educate and inspire others to aspire to have jeong in their lives.

With Then I Met You, I also wanted to dive deep into the product development process because building jeong with your craft leads to a more meaningful relationship with your work. Whether it was the decision to include a high concentration of antioxidant seaberries or perfecting the velvet texture of the Living Cleansing Balm, I wanted to be involved in a way that mirrored my commitment to going deeper in everything I did.

Soko Glam is now the largest leading Korean beauty platform with millions of customers coming to shop and learn about skin care every month. Meanwhile, Then I Met You has already won 12 industry awards, though we're only two years old and have only six products. To this day, I sometimes struggle to believe that we were able to upend an industry by introducing K-beauty to the U.S. and creating a market that now brings in revenues of over

$5.6 billion a year. But as I look back, I credit the power of jeong with changing my life and my perspective. It has given me the motivation to do what I am passionate about, even if it isn't the most popular direction or if I'm faced with some of the hardest days.

Dave and I have received our fair share of awards and recognition thus far in our journey—from *Forbes*, *CNN*, *Fast Company*, and other high-profile outlets—but the only piece we've ever hung on our wall is a plaque from a small government organization that no one has likely heard of. It reads, "Charlotte & Dave Cho. In recognition of their outstanding contributions to the United States and Korean-American community." To us, it's the most meaningful by far. Just a simple reminder that we're on the right track and grounded in what drives us each and every day—jeong.

Simple Acts of Jeong

- *If you have an entrepreneurial spirit,* but you're not sure where to begin, start by figuring out your passions— what or who do you have jeong with? Write down a list of those deep connections and why you feel so strongly about them. Any one of them could spark your new venture.

- *If you're lacking self-motivation,* feel lazy, or even lost, keeping a jeong list could also motivate you to achieve goals you never thought possible. For example, if you have jeong with your parents, it could inspire you to save more money so that you can treat them to a nice vacation or financially care for them if they need the support when they retire. In my experience, being internally motivated by something outside of yourself will bring you the most fulfillment.

Chapter 5

The Power to Give Without
Expecting Anything in Return

AFTER LEARNING ABOUT JEONG AND ITS CONTEX-tual importance in Korean society, I had actively started to see it at work during my daily life in Seoul. It was constantly referenced in pop culture like *Misaeng: Incomplete Life* (one of my favorite Korean dramas because it reminds me of office life in Seoul). I also witnessed moments of jeong between two people and even groups of people. Once our team took a bus several hours from Seoul to a remote countryside village to pay our respects when a teammate's family member had passed. Eventually, I began to see how jeong was playing a role in my own life. As I shared in the last chapter, my jeong for Korea is what gave me the courage to start Soko Glam when I had always felt lost and otherwise uninspired in the past. Jeong made me zero in on what was important—finding and building deep connections—and that kept me grounded and invested in the things that mattered.

This made me want to cultivate more jeong in my own

life, even after Dave and I moved to New York. Over the years, I had been eager to share the values of jeong with others around me, but just as it had been difficult for my Korean colleagues to explain the concept, naturally it was difficult for me. Most people I talked to simply assumed jeong was just another word for love, which is not entirely accurate.

To me, the word love has lost meaning over time due to its casual and liberal use. For example, you can say "love" to show how much you enjoy something—"I love double cleansing!"—and you'll see it on many comment threads—"Love this!"—followed by a few sparkling emoji hearts, as a way to show support.

In comparison, the phrase "이러다 정 들겠어" (ee-ruh-dah-jeong-deul-get-suh), which translates to "if this goes on, we may develop jeong," is used when a person is starting to grow on you and foreshadows that a deeper connection will be made. Or "정이 무섭다" (jeong-ee mu-sub-da), which translates to "jeong is scary" and is a common expression that describes the lengths people will go in the name of jeong. These are just a few examples of how jeong is used—instead of the word love—to indicate a different feeling.

Another point: Love, sad to say, can be short-lived. You can fall quickly in love and then back out, whereas jeong is forever—whether you like it or not. Unlike the fleeting emotion that love can be, jeong is about acknowledging and respecting the impact that a person, place, or thing has made on your life. If you were to have a falling out with a family member or break up with a significant other, you would have fallen out of love, but the jeong you cultivated during your time together would remain. As I previously explained, *miweon* jeong means that you often miss the connection you once had with a friend when they're no longer around, even if you had grown to dislike each other over time.

The Korean-American author Jenny Han described it well in her novel *P.S. I Still Love You*. (It was referenced in the Netflix adaptation, too!) Writing through her female protagonist, Lara Jean, she explains, "There's a Korean word my grandma taught me. It's called [jeong]. It's the connection between two people that can't be severed, even when love turns to hate. You still have those old feelings for them; you can't ever completely shake them loose of you; you will always have tenderness in your heart for them."

The Downside of Jeong

Sometimes jeong can be manipulated to become a powerful negative force. You might feel unnecessarily indebted to someone, or you might feel pressured to do something morally wrong because of an existing relationship. Jeong is so powerful that Korean companies like Samsung sometimes forbid workers from the same schools or hometowns from holding official meetings to prevent any favors being done for each other based on the jeong they may have.

There's also a phrase, "정 때문에 산다 (jeong-ttae-moon-ae-san-da), which means "they're just living together because of jeong" and is used to describe a person that is living for or living with someone based purely on their shared history. When taken to extremes, this can indicate someone living their life with blind loyalty (such as someone in an abusive relationship with their partner), which is another example of when jeong is far from positive.

These are two examples of when jeong, a good thing, can go wrong. The important thing is to remember that jeong doesn't mean to blindly follow your feelings, but to set limits for yourself. When things feel wrong to the point where you're uncomfortable or you're being harassed, speak up, and if necessary, seek help from someone you trust.

Remember that having jeong with someone also means not being afraid to be firm and say no. If there truly is jeong between you, they will be open-minded and respect your thoughts, then together, you can learn and grow from the understandings that have been built. If they don't respect that? Life is short, and you'll want to invest in building connections that enrich your life. The fact is that sometimes you'll have to cut a few bad ties to make room for relationships that matter.

Why Jeong Is Deeper Than Love

Another key detail that sets jeong apart from love is that romance does not have to be part of the equation. Think of an important person in your life who you haven't dated, but you'd do anything for—you've probably been through thick and thin together. That's what defines jeong: the understanding you have of one another that was built through shared hardships and celebrations.

Take Mr. Hong, the vice president that I worked with at Samsung for five years, who has been a mentor and someone I've cultivated jeong with over our 10-year history. Under his leadership and careful guidance, I gained the confidence to pursue many challenging projects. As a 26-year-old associate, for instance, I was put on a task force to execute a million-dollar grand-opening event in Saudi Arabia that involved our company CEO and even a few Saudi princes. I couldn't have done it without his constant support.

But he was not just a good manager and mentor. At 20-plus years my senior, he became more like a second father. During the holidays, like *Chuseok* (Korean Thanksgiving) or *Seollal* (Lunar New Year's Day), he invited me to his own family gatherings since mine were far away. When my parents finally came to visit me in Korea, he made it a point to meet them and take them out to dinner. He was so kind and we worked so well together that my other colleagues would tease that I was like his daughter.

Somehow it was easy to build jeong with Mr. Hong. He was naturally empathetic and freely gave me his time when I lived in Korea. Perhaps it was because he had two daughters of his own, and both of them had plans to study abroad in the U.S. He knew what it meant to be alone in a new country without much family to rely on, so in many ways, he was able to understand me and made the extra effort. Looking back, I realize his generosity was exactly what I needed at that time, living halfway across the world from my own family and in a country where I could hardly speak the language. Pushing through those hardships cemented the relationship we still have today.

When it was finally time for me to go, I struggled with the thought of leaving Korea and everyone else in it behind. Mr. Hong tried his best to console me. "You know you could always develop your career further by staying here, while Dave goes to school in New York," he told me. "After Dave finishes his MBA, he can apply for Samsung and have an opportunity to continue living in Korea."

But only two years later, Dave and I would be the ones to invite Mr. Hong to be part of our crazy journey.

Jeong Means Paying It Forward

When you're starting something (like a business) from scratch, trust me—you're going to need all the help you can get. Luckily, Dave and I were fortunate to have people around us who were willing to go the extra mile from the beginning.

We planted the first seeds for Soko Glam while we were still living in Seoul. I spent a few months meeting wholesale distributors and scouring stores to procure products that we kept stocked in the closet of our Itaewon apartment. Our site went live from our apartment, just two months after Dave received his acceptance letter. It was only the two of us running this operation, fulfilling online orders from our home and shipping out of our neighborhood post office.

By the time we launched in December, we had only a few months remaining—four to be exact—before we had to move back to the States. As a two-person married team, we knew that keeping Soko Glam alive and running while we were packing up our entire lives would be an enormous logistical challenge, to say the least. Thankfully, our friend Lily jumped in to save the day.

Lily and I had a long history together—and lots of jeong. We met in junior high, but didn't become close until we both went to UC Irvine. Our friendship blossomed during our college years: We lived in the same Mesa dorms freshman year, and we happily crammed ourselves into an apartment with four other girls the following year. She was the one I turned to whenever I grew homesick in Korea. Every day we would hop on Google Chat, and she would update me on all the goings-on. We spent hours talking about everything, even the most mundane topics like what we ate for lunch and what phone we planned to upgrade to. I believe I have jeong with Lily not only for the good times we shared, but because she's someone who will tell me the truth, even when I don't want to hear it. I truly believe these authentic and hard conversations are an essential component for jeong on both sides. (I'll talk more about this in a later chapter!)

Lily was living in New York at the time, and it didn't take me more than a moment to think to ask her for help. That's the nice thing about jeong between people—it's never one-sided, and you don't hesitate to ask for help because you know that you would do the same if the roles were reversed. Within days, Lily was set up as our operator and fulfillment center, receiving a mini-warehouse full of goods in her tiny Brooklyn apartment, and our problems were solved. If it hadn't been for her willingness to do this, we would have had to shut down operations for a couple of weeks while we moved from Seoul to NYC, and who knows where that would have led us.

When I look back at our journey, Danny is another friend who gave without expecting anything in return. We became friends after meeting at a wedding in Korea and spent a lot of time gallivanting around gay bars and clubs in Itaewon together. We lost touch when he moved to New York in 2011, but after Dave and I moved there too, we started connecting in real life again. (With all jeong-based friendships, time and distance mean nothing!)

Danny came to our aid when we were hit by a legal letter from a company during our first year. I was brand new to business and had no clue how to handle legal issues, so even though it was a standard intimidation tactic (I later discovered it was unfortunately common in business), it worked on me. It even affected some of our relationships, as that company continued on and contacted our partners directly with false claims, and I worried that our reputation would suffer due to their aggressive actions.

Danny was working at a top law firm that we would have never been able to afford at the time, but he came to our rescue by taking time out of his busy schedule to help us respond smartly, pro bono. They never bothered us again, and we had him to thank. We were so small at the time and certainly couldn't afford to spend thousands on legal counsel. With nothing to gain, Danny helped us when we needed it most.

I quickly learned this life lesson: Sometimes, all you need to do is ask. Everyone needs help once in a while, and having jeong means you give and receive unconditional support. In the last eight years, there have been so many people who were willing to give. Now, no matter how busy we get, we remind ourselves daily how important it is to pay it forward too.

Simple Acts of Jeong

Support a Small Business and Become a Regular

As much as Amazon, Walmart, and Whole Foods make it convenient for me to get groceries and buy batteries (and really, really cheap underwear), there is something soulless about *only* engaging with those brands. That's why I make it a point to shop at a small business or support a local restaurant at least once a week because they have something the big brands don't often have—and that's human connection.

I think food tastes significantly more delicious when someone that has put their livelihood and passions on the line is making it. That's why I love frequenting hole-in-the-wall restaurants: They're like hidden gems that satisfy more than just your hunger. To be frank, I find some of that magic is lost when you're dining at a place that only cares about the bottom line or treats its customers like a number.

The same feeling applies to small shops, whose products can be just as high quality as the brand name versions. In fact, the experience is often better when the small business owner truly cares about their community and customers in a more personal way than a large corporation can ever do at scale. It's especially apparent to me, as an independent business owner who cares about my community as well.

I feel rewarded when I am able to establish a rapport (or with time, jeong!) with people at my local restaurants and shops. As a regular, I'll get to know their name and sometimes even their kids' names; they'll know exactly what I want to order and they'll even save the seat that they know I prefer. In return, I love knowing that my regular patronage helps their business run. Getting to know them as people, and not as a service that I pay for, makes them eventually feel like family, and that's priceless.

The Business Trip

Toward the end of 2013, Soko Glam started to gain traction, and Dave and I decided to take it to the "next level." That meant forming relationships directly with the brands that we curated, instead of working through our wholesale vendor, as well as connecting with brands that we wanted to curate in the future by meeting them face-to-face. In other words, we would be taking a business trip to Korea.

My excitement began to build because it felt like a sign that Soko Glam had become more than a side gig. It would be my first time back to Korea since we had moved, and I could practically taste the *patbingsoo* (sweet red bean on shaved ice) with a condensed milk drizzle and fresh fruit and mochi on top (my favorite Korean frozen treat).

I knew it would be different, though, because I was no longer a resident of Seoul. Dave also wouldn't be coming with me since he was a full-time student at Columbia, and he had to take care of running the day-to-day of Soko Glam back in New York. (It was still just the two of us!) So I asked Ron, our mutual friend, if I could stay at his place in Seoul since he had an extra bedroom. Dave and I had no salary between the two of us (and one of us was a full-time student), and we were living in one of the most expensive cities in the world with a business that was burning more money than it was making. We would take whatever help we could get.

I was nervous, though. The goal of the trip was to meet and successfully convince multiple brands to work with Soko Glam directly, so that we could cut out the middle man. There were also several brands that our wholesale vendor did not stock at all, so I had been buying them at-cost in stores; I didn't care about profit margins, only about having the best curation. Direct partnerships would mean that we would get the latest samples and be able to make exciting launches on our site with the best pricing for our customers. I knew that with direct access, I'd be able to speak to the brands about the ingredients and the formulas to ensure my curation was top-notch.

I badly wanted to curate these brands like Banila Co. and Skinfood, which were already well-known throughout Asia. But Soko Glam was still relatively unknown and had no track record to lean on, so I knew it would be a challenge. Particularly, I was nervous about conducting these meetings in real life. My open and embarrassing secret was that despite having lived in Korea for so long, my Korean fluency remained at the elementary-school level.

So I called Mr. Hong. Even though it had been almost a year since we had last spoken, I didn't hesitate to message him on KakaoTalk, Korea's go-to messaging app. I wanted to know more about Korean business etiquette, so that I could better prepare for these meetings, as well as the best way to travel to them, as many of them would be held on the outskirts of Seoul in places I had never been. He was always wise—my one-stop mentor!—and I trusted his advice. I had heard through the grapevine that shortly after I had left, he had retired from Samsung. Typically, employees will devote several decades to climbing up the ladder at a single company, and when their tenure ends around age 50, most begin their "second life" at new jobs, becoming top executives at smaller companies or launching their own business ventures. It had been about half a year since then.

"Mr. Hong? How are you?" I wrote.

"Charlotte, it's so surprising to hear from you," he responded in Korean. "It's been a long time—how are you?"

"I'm good. I just wanted to let you know I'm coming back to Korea for a trip!"

"Oh really, so soon! We should get some of the team together and have dinner."

"That would be nice, I would love that." I continued on, "Mr. Hong . . . I heard you've left Samsung."

"Yes, that's right," he wrote. "I'm retired now and enjoying my break."

"That's great, I hope you are finally getting to rest."

"I am, I'm reading more . . . I'm finally traveling. It's good."

I nodded and smiled. I was happy for him. It was time to tell him what I'd been up to.

"By the way, I don't know if you've heard, but Dave and I started a company called Soko Glam curating Korean cosmetics," I explained. "It's a small business, but it's starting to pick up."

"Oh, that's interesting. Is it going well?" he asked.

"I'm going to Korea because I'm going to meet with some potential brands. I was wondering if you knew the best way to get to Gyeonggi-do. It's for a meeting I have with a mask brand."

"Hmm, that's pretty far from Seoul," he wrote back. "There aren't subways that go there directly."

"Yea . . . that's what I thought."

"Why don't I take you?" he offered. "It won't be easy to get there unless you have a car."

"Are you sure?" I asked. "I don't want to bother you."

"It's no bother. I'm not busy right now anyway."

"Really? OK, thank you! Thank you so much Mr. Hong."

I would never have dreamed of asking him for that much—not only to drive me, but to attend the meeting by my side—but just like that, he gave me his time.

Just 24 hours after I landed in Seoul, Mr. Hong picked me up at Jamsil subway station to head to our first meeting, and we caught up as he drove. It turned out that the place I was trying to go was not only inaccessible by subway, it was two hours away near a manufacturing plant where they actually produced most of the sheet masks. As we left the concrete jungle of Seoul and the countryside whizzed by, I breathed a little easier knowing that Mr. Hong was coming with me.

We parked in a dusty lot and were quickly greeted by In-Jae, the friendly sales associate that I had been conversing with over email for the past few weeks. I was interested in a few high-quality sheet masks I had tried from his line, which was an affordable private label (I learned that their company manufactured masks for several premium skin care brands). I knew I wanted to curate them on Soko Glam, and he had been quite receptive to my emails. Meeting face-to-face, I tried not to seem too eager, so that he wouldn't realize it was my first official meeting.

In the conference room, there was a little tray of refreshments—orange juice, grape juice, cookies—and a presentation deck laid out for us. As the other team members entered, they each bowed and provided their business cards. I thankfully was prepared with my own set of Soko Glam cards, knowing this was the way Korean business was conducted thanks to my years at Samsung. Mr. Hong obviously didn't have any to hand out, which made them even more curious about why he was part of the meeting at all.

The brand presented their slides, explaining how their sheet masks had won multiple awards, and began to distribute an array of samples that would demonstrate their quality. Throughout the meeting, I couldn't help but be so thankful that Mr. Hong had come with me. Unless the topic was food, I could not conduct an entire business meeting with my level of fluency.

On top of that, he brought a lot of credibility to Soko Glam because of his age and status, which mattered in Korea's hierarchical society. When he told them that he was a former VP of Samsung, I noticed the nods of approval from around the room. With Mr. Hong at the table, it suddenly made our new company a tad more trustworthy in their eyes. There was (and is still) a fair amount of stereotyping in Korea's business world, and I know it would have looked a lot less professional if a 27-year-old *gyopo* (a person of Korean descent with a foreign citizenship) had been there alone.

On the car ride back to Seoul, I expressed my relief that the first official business meeting for Soko Glam had gone better than I expected. I started rattling off the next steps on what Dave and I needed to do next, from negotiating the contract to figuring out how I would export these items. Mr. Hong was oddly quiet. Finally, after a long pause, he said in Korean, "Honestly, I was confused halfway through the presentation. This whole time I thought I was taking you to a 'mask' factory, like the ones you cover your nose and mouth with at dental or medical offices. I was so confused when they were showing face packs, the sheet masks that my wife wears!"

We started laughing hysterically in the car. It suddenly occurred to me that he knew very little about my business. He hadn't even known who we were meeting, but it hadn't mattered. He had only known it had been important to me and had wanted to help. This sheet mask revelation in the car is one of my favorite memories and still a story we tell to others over drinks.

Mr. Hong's foray into the beauty world didn't end there. He proved to be even more valuable as my trip went on.

He decided to accompany me to all the other meetings I had lined up that week. When I returned home to New York, he continued to help me and Dave for months. He pitched Soko Glam to new brands and helped get them on-board. Using his supply chain background (10 years at Samsung!), he helped manage the logistics of exporting Korean beauty products to the U.S. per FDA regulations. He helped check our inventory and match them up with order numbers, and he even networked and pushed for press coverage in the Korean newspapers. At the time, with our company barely fueling itself off of our savings and without having raised any capital, things were tight— and he continued to help us pro bono. He thought the work was enjoyable, and he knew we needed his help from time to time, which he was happy to do.

Although he was brand new to the industry, his location in Korea and his business background were invaluable. Despite his lack of beauty knowledge and the small size of our company, he was able to convince so many brands to be a part of the Soko Glam curation. After a few months of working together, it felt like a no-brainer to offer Mr. Hong a full-time position as the head of our Korea office—our first hire to Soko Glam.

Thinking With Your Heart, Not With Your Head

If you think my story with Mr. Hong is unique, you're right, it is. If you know anything about Korean society and cultural norms, then you'll know that I believe it's almost unprecedented for a Korean man with his background to come work for a former subordinate at a startup. (It's probably why the movie *The Intern* with Anne Hathaway and Robert De Niro was such a hit in South Korea. Everyone was so intrigued by the idea of a 70-year-old man working as an intern at a fashion start-up.) And let's not forget that joining Soko Glam meant deciding to forgo other opportunities, turning down lucrative job offers to go all in.

His meaningful choice ignited something inside of me, and it made me feel like working 10,000 times harder than I already was. Knowing that Mr. Hong was putting his career and reputation on the line made it more important for me to ensure it was all worth it for him. It was something beyond my own personal gain, similar to how I felt about shouldering responsibility for my parents and my team. For them, I *had* to make Soko Glam a success and a place to be proud to work.

Years later, the executives that had thought he was crazy for coming to Soko Glam were applauding his foresight. "How'd you know to get into Korean beauty?" they'd poke and prod him over a catch-up dinner. I don't have to ask Mr. Hong if he knew. He didn't, and neither did Dave or I. His decision wasn't based on industry trends, on a lucrative salary, or on clout. He was thinking with his heart, more than his head. It was jeong.

Follow Your Heart

Thinking with your heart, more than your head, can be beneficial for you personally *and* professionally, even when you may think you're giving more than you're receiving. The truth is that the relationships you have are the key to earning many life-changing opportunities, and by being as helpful and kind as possible to those around you, you'll be rewarded with deep relationships with people who are genuinely rooting for your success.

The secret is to be proactive and *not* expect anything in return. Whether it's giving advice, making a mutual connection, or celebrating someone's wins, simply taking the time out of your day to support others will help you solidify that connection. It's a no-brainer—being kind and considerate goes a long way.

As I shared in this chapter, I've been lucky to have a strong group of people support me with Soko Glam and Then I Met You. I never felt that they were helping me because they felt they owed me or wanted something from me, but because they genuinely wished to see me do well. There were those who took time out of their busy day to walk me through how to register a business, survey potential customers, share different e-commerce and fulfillment options, and give me legal advice.

When I was new to New York and had no personal beauty contacts, I met one editor, Annie, who after a single meeting, was kind enough to introduce me to her contacts in the space. For every beauty editor I met, I tried to be as helpful as possible. If they needed to speak with a Korean R&D specialist or they needed something translated from Korean to English for their skin care story, I was there to assist by linking them to my contacts in Korea or by doing the translation myself. It didn't matter if they needed help on something that didn't directly benefit me, nor did I ever demand that they write a story about Soko Glam in exchange—I was just trying to be as helpful as I could. Since we were colleagues in the same industry (obviously with similar interests), many of them ended up becoming friends, as we built jeong with each other outside of work.

On the flip side, if you're hypercompetitive and constantly weighing if your support is going to personally benefit you in some way, your view of the world and your relationships will be hopelessly shallow. Only looking out for yourself, taking all the credit to accelerate your position, or seeing relationships as an equal exchange of favors won't lead to much at all.

Those who genuinely wish to help others—without expecting anything in return—will have better reputations, stronger relationships, and a larger network. They'll be introduced to the people in their lives that truly love being with them. I know from personal experience that 99 percent of entrepreneurship is about perseverance, and you'll need to surround yourself with the strongest support system you can to survive. So get started with the basics! Something as simple as a warm smile and staying present in all your conversations (yes, put your phone away!) will be the first step to establishing those important relationships.

Chapter 6

Jeong Takes Time

I GREW UP IN THE SUBURBS OF LOS ANGELES COUNTY: First in Whittier, and then once I hit sixth grade, I moved to Hacienda Heights, a small town nearby. Life was quiet in the suburbs. Too quiet. An exciting night out involved a visit to a chain restaurant, like a TGI Friday's or a Baja Fresh, in a cookie-cutter strip mall. To get around, my only viable option was to drive my parents' 1998 Volvo with old leather seats that were starting to peel and curl up from the dry California sun. L.A. County was too sprawling for my taste—public transit was not an effective mode of transport—and to see anything worthwhile, you'd spend an hour or two stuck in traffic, a line of red tail lights snaking up for miles on the 605 Freeway.

When I turned 18, it was like a switch had flipped, and suddenly I started to crave city life. In college, I took a weekend trip out to New York with my roommate, Jean, and two of my former coworkers (I worked at an independent movie theater my freshman year), and it made me imagine what it might be like to actually live in a city with such high energy. In our own sleeping bags, we crashed on the floor of our coworker's friend's East Village apartment. It was the dead of winter, with snow up to our shins, and we barely wore any clothes to shield us from it, but everything was so exhilarating that it didn't matter. During the day I navigated the subway system. One time I made the mistake of taking it during rush hour and was spun in circles by the rush of Wall Street commuters with their long, black coats and steel-eyed expressions, dashing to grab their next transfer.

Above ground I was greeted by food carts and pigeons crowding the already narrow sidewalks, and I peered into all the clever boutiques and restaurants that I wished I had more time to explore. In the few nights I was there, I went to my first launch party for an arts magazine and managed to befriend a bunch of rambunctious college kids at a bar in St. Marks. I knew just from that one weekend that it would be my dream to live in NYC, colliding with a group of diverse people from all walks of life who were equally drawn to it. Coming from a small city, I thought it would be amazing to be surrounded by and feel connected to so many people each and every day. Luckily, before I finally made it to New York, I got the added bonus of living in the equally dynamic city of Seoul first.

Surprisingly, it wasn't love at first sight in either case. It took me about one year in Seoul to get over the culture shock and work toward a more meaningful connection with the city. When I moved to New York, it took almost two years of exploring neighborhoods and building memories and friendships to find that deeper connection. Although I did grow to love them both, I discovered that living in two densely populated cities was not entirely what I had expected. We were literally stacked on top of each other in the tallest skyscrapers in the world, packed like sardines on New York's L train or in Seoul's Gangnam Station, which made me feel more small and insignificant. Instead of experiencing an intense feeling of community with those all around me, there were times I felt more alone than ever before.

In Seoul, with its population of around 10 million, I'm embarrassed to admit that I never learned any of my neighbors' names in the five years I lived there, something I had done more successfully while living in Southern California. I couldn't even blame it on the language barrier because living in New York City, with its population of over eight million people, was no different. Dave and I stayed at the same apartment in Flatiron for four years, and I never gave more than a nod and a smile to my neighbors as we passed each other in the elevators or in the hallways. I lived in other neighborhoods: the Upper West Side, then finally Williamsburg, and it was all pretty much the same. Only slivers of proof hinted at our shared existence, like discarded recyclables in the refuse room or hurried footsteps through the hallway. I knew they were there, living with us on the same apartment floors, but I didn't have a name, let alone a relationship, even though we all were within a few hundred square feet of each other.

Then there has been the rise of social media in the last decade. I'm no sociologist, but I'm guessing that technology hasn't helped us in this department. The intention behind platforms like Facebook, Instagram and TikTok is to make the world more open and connected. Instead, when I'm on them, I often feel more distant. There's something alienating about scrolling through manicured pictures from the safety of our smartphones. Having straddled both the pre-tech and post-tech ages, I can see through the facade of social media. Hours of lounging around each other's rooms, quietly listening to a new album together and confiding your secrets, have now been replaced by endless TikTok dance challenges. I saw the progression: In-person meetings were replaced by long phone conversations, which then became emails. Somehow even those have now been reduced to text exchanges—either DMs (direct messages) or phone messages—that are usually no more than 300 characters long. While efficient, it provides a false sense of connection: You think you're up-to-date on the lives of the people you care about, but you haven't cared to hear the details firsthand.

Although I love my Instagram community for being so supportive and am thankful that I can communicate with everyone in real time, in retrospect, I've also felt like a passive observer with no real depth or foundation to build upon. I feel the second and third order effects of being on these platforms: laziness and plain social apathy. Compared to my life before I moved to these bustling cities, I somehow spend more time on my own. Instead of putting myself out there to build quality connections, whether by making concrete plans to catch up over dinner or even just have a proper phone call, I'm "too busy" stuck at home, face buried in my cell phone, repeatedly hitting that refresh button.

While I belong to the social media generation—I joined Facebook when I was a freshman in college—I am wistful for the days when even pagers were considered a novelty. Staying in touch was less convenient, but there was something more nourishing about the relationships that you built naturally, as you focused on quality over quantity. It does take more effort to call a friend to meet in person, but the effort is rewarded with something that is priceless: jeong.

It's one of the reasons why I am fascinated with *Reply 1988*, which is my favorite Korean drama without a doubt. I watched it when it first aired in 2015, three years into our Soko Glam journey, and I remember eagerly waiting each week for a new episode. Yes, I had watched dozens of dramas before it, but there was something different about this one—even Dave got into it, and he *never* gets into dramas. *Reply 1988* is set in a small town in the mid-1980s and centers on the lives of six families in a close-knit community, reminiscent of what one might see in a traditional village. They all live on the same block, and there's no modern-day technology to distract them or keep them "connected." They formed bonds just by spending quality time with each other. From illnesses to money woes, high school crushes to graduations, these families experienced—and most importantly, shared—everything together.

In particular, food is shared again and again throughout the entire 20-episode series (the potent jeong-builder we discussed in detail in Chapter 3). Every family would cook extra-large portions of their dishes, then without hesitation, package up the excess for their kids to deliver platter by platter to their neighbors. In the end, everyone benefited: Although each family might have prepared only one recipe, they always sat down to a wide variety of delicious dishes, courtesy of their collective. No one on the show went without, not even the one family without a maternal figure (the wife and mother had died at a young age). The little community operated as one unit, navigating the intricacies of life together and treating each other with care, like one big extended family.

Watching *Reply 1988* from our New York apartment, I craved that camaraderie and the friendly neighborhood atmosphere. The level of comfort and care that I saw on screen was starkly different from anything I had felt in my entire 35 years of existence, but it made me realize that as humans it is our instinct to empathize and support one another. It may be naive for me to think that it's possible to operate like a village in the 21st century, when we're all trained to chase instant gratification and carry the false belief that happiness and success happen overnight (I blame Amazon Prime!). But it still doesn't make me want it any less.

Time Well Spent

Thanks to the Internet, apps, social media, and smartphones, we are distracted 24/7 by technology. According to a 2019 global digital report from Hootsuite and We Are Social, studies show we now spend a whopping six hours and 42 minutes online each day, half of which is on mobile devices. If you do the math, that's more than 27 percent of every year. A slew of researchers have conducted studies that associate this increased Internet usage (mainly on social networking sites) with increased rates of depression, anxiety, insomnia, and low self-esteem, not to mention the effect it has had on our general social skills. Personally, I find my phone to be a source of distraction all day and feel as if I am exchanging jeong-building time with real humans for a hunk of plastic. So what can we do about it?

• To minimize your screen time and make more people time, try living by a "digital sunset" and get off your phone once the sun goes down. Don't bring it into your bedroom; charge it where it's out of sight. This removes the temptation to check your phone before you go to sleep and to reach for it when you wake up. If you're using your phone as an alarm, simply get a separate alarm clock for your bedside.

• Download one of the many apps that monitor your social media usage like AppDetox, AntiSocial, Social Fever, and AppBlock (new iPhones even have a built-in Screen Time tracking function). They help to curb your bad habits and to be conscious of the time you spend on your phone, so you don't go overboard.

• All that said, there's no need to log off completely—just use your time wisely. Technology has done a lot of good things too. It's paved the way for more accessible mental health services, including therapy apps and digital meditation tools like Headspace. It has helped spread knowledge about social and political injustices. And it creates opportunities to connect with communities of like-minded people—like the K-beauty community, for one—whom you might never have been able to meet otherwise. On a personal note, I'm thankful to have a platform where I can share my views and impact positive change as an Asian-American.

Showing Your Full Self

As much as I'd like to entirely blame technology for my difficulties forging jeong—or at least a working relationship with my neighbors—it's not the only reason why it's difficult today. A big stepping stone to building jeong is the ability to show your full self. By that, I mean that we need to be comfortable being real and imperfect. Lately, we've been conditioned to only want to show our best selves, carefully documented on a three-by-three grid, even when reality doesn't match up.

Not long after we launched Soko Glam, when I started sharing my public persona on Instagram, I felt pressured to post nothing but picturesque brunch spreads and chic, enviable outfits. According to conventional wisdom, I was a founder of a beauty company and needed to project my aspirational life as a "girl boss." But the reality was that I was nowhere near enjoying mid-day brunches in Chelsea with my girlfriends. Instead, I was barely surviving on a few cups of coffee for an entire day, head down, working through the daily grind with the team. Not only did I not have the budget to sustain a designer wardrobe, I was more known in the office and among my close friends and family as the type of person to stain a white jean jacket with a dollop of ketchup that had missed my mouth. In all honesty, my full self was a frazzled cofounder of Soko Glam, insecure about my speaking abilities and my general ability to measure up to traditional beauty industry standards.

I'm not saying that building jeong means *not* sharing the picture-perfect wins in your life. Of course there are plenty of joys in celebrating your unexpected raise, your 21st birthday, or the dog you just adopted. But jeong requires you to be real: about the moments when you had a falling out with your mom or the time you cried after your heart was broken. This includes the test you failed, the job interview you bombed, or the unbearable grief felt when a family member passes. These are all a part of life, but they don't seem to have a place in our "personal brands" as seen on social media.

The silver lining is that every bump in the road helps build the strongest bonds. Are they going to understand your pain and listen when you need to vent? Will they be there when you need someone the most? I truly believe you won't know for certain until that person sees every side of you.

The Jeong We Built

Looking back at my journey of building Soko Glam with Dave, I can tell you that there are many ups and downs to starting a company—especially when you are starting from scratch and even more so when you are bootstrapped with no safety net. Unlike the happy highlight reels you get from reading an article or listening to a podcast about entrepreneurship, it's actually not all that glamorous. Throw in the fact that you're a husband and wife cofounding team without any prior experience running a company and trust me—a lot of the ups and downs will bleed into your personal life too.

"Charlotte, I'd be very careful going into business with a spouse. I've seen brothers who go into business together get torn apart." I remember hearing this advice from a friend on a cold winter day in Seoul, 2012, when Dave and I were just getting started with Soko Glam. Naturally, I disregarded their advice with a chuckle and an eye-roll. At that point, it was more of a fun weekend passion project. How much strain would this "business" be to our relationship?

If you had told me then that a decade later, I would be

sitting next to Dave, still working together on not one, but several brands, I would have never believed you. Despite all of our compatibility, we couldn't be more different. I am a free spirit and fiercely liberal; I am also (quite) messy and (a bit) disorganized. Take a peek in our closet, and you'll see piles of my clothes strewn about (to me, it's my organized mess). Dave, on the other hand, has his color-coded shirts hung neatly on wooden hangers spaced equally apart and perfectly canted. He is extremely neat and orderly. When he cooks (which is 99 percent of the time), he chops his onions and tomatoes with such precision that they look like the lines on grid paper. When I cook, the spices and dried noodles explode like an actual flavor bomb. He has a memory like an elephant, yet I can't remember if I've shampooed my hair in the shower. He is good at math, process-oriented, and sharp with the details. Meanwhile, I have a knack for creative projects and ideas.

Needless to say we don't always see eye to eye. In the early years of Soko Glam, when we were living in a small apartment on the Upper West Side, we decided to sell most of our furniture—the TV, the TV stand, his bike—to make room for all the inventory we had to fulfill between the two of us. Once, we got into a heated debate over the way I had taped up a box. Noting that I had taped the exterior *clear tape* crookedly, Dave retaped everything before we hand-delivered it to the post office. Everything, and I mean *everything*, pointed to the idea that we would never work well together.

Our journey has been far from perfect, and we've made a lot of mistakes along the way that were agonizing and downright stressful. If you've ever worked with a significant other, or even a family member, you'll know how easy it is to push each other's buttons over the smallest things. In a professional setting, one wouldn't react or say certain things to a colleague, but when you're family, anything and everything is fair game. Simple disagreements would escalate into full-on shouting matches.

But despite the challenges, it was equally beautiful to experience because in growing our company, we truly saw each other's full selves. We celebrated together when we were able to get an editor so enthused about K-beauty that we landed coverage in *Elle* magazine, without the help of an expensive PR agency. (At the time, K-beauty was so far from mainstream that some people initially thought I was referring to Kardashian beauty.) We leaned on each other when a huge warehouse fiasco left us scrambling to respond to thousands of customers who experienced delayed shipments of their orders. We persisted together, like the time we were able to convince a prominent beauty brand to trust us, even though we didn't speak Korean fluently and didn't yet have a track record. Every milestone felt that much greater because we saw our hard work pay off together.

Over the years, I learned to trust him deeply, and we pooled our strengths to grow the company. As the face of the company, much of the credit goes to me by default, but the truth is, a lot of our success has been contingent on his guidance and leadership, a true CEO. Although he is out of the spotlight, he has steered the team through challenges and has persevered in building an innovative platform. Where I didn't excel, he filled in the gaps. He had a point about the straight tape: Those details matter when it comes to making happy customers, and his maniacal focus on the customer would build a strong brand built on trust. And even though he works behind the scenes and his contributions aren't public knowledge, he never complains or looks for the limelight.

We joke to our friends and colleagues that although we

have been married for over a decade, working together all these years makes it feel like three times that. In truth, we're not joking—it does feel like we've been together for so much longer because Dave has seen every side of me. He has seen the good: my excitement over our first order, the book deal, the plans I have to take care of my family. He's also seen me at my most vulnerable, when I saw my mom suffer from delusions during a period of high stress, or when I simply broke down from feeling insecure and out of place. There were so many moments when I told him I was simply not capable.

He is there at all times, to laugh at my bad jokes and to actively work to take things off my plate when I get over-whelmed. But he also pushes me, coaches me, and encourages me to do the things that I always swore I could not do. And though I hate to admit it, I've reached new levels of potential I never knew I had because of him.

There is no one I have more jeong with in this world than Dave. His role in my life is deeper than just that of a cofounder, husband, or a best friend. I have also been there for his greatest and toughest moments, and I try my best to support and challenge him. This is the unimaginable gift God has given us.

Meeting Michelle

The same "show your full self" rule doesn't only apply to your significant other or someone you spend a lot of time with. There are moments where showing your full self to a stranger could lead to a relationship filled with jeong.

In 2017, I was introduced to Michelle Phan—the YouTube star who paved the way for all beauty influencers—through Jennifer, a mutual friend of ours. I met Jennifer when she was working at Ipsy, a monthly beauty subscription company, and she invited me to collaborate on a special Korean beauty set for their Girl Boss collection (we also clicked over our love for Korean dramas and beauty). She told me I would get along with Michelle, and though Jennifer said that she normally didn't make introductions, she felt strongly about getting us together in a room. The next time that Dave and I went to visit L.A., where Michelle lived, we had the chance to meet in person.

I was nervous. Before I was involved in beauty, I had been an early follower of Michelle's YouTube videos. I stumbled upon her channel because she was one of the few posting beauty content at the time, and I was instantly drawn to her soothing voice and approachability. Michelle's knack for creating flawless makeup tutorials eventually translated into several business ventures, which made me respect her on another level. She had locked in an official brand deal with L'Oréal called EM, and then she cofounded Ipsy, a successful beauty subscription company based in Silicon Valley. Of course I knew nothing about her in detail, only what I had read about her in articles and interviews and from what I could see on her social media channels.

I remember walking down the corridor to the conference room at her Ipsy office. On the way, I saw photos of Michelle on the cover of several prestigious magazines like *Forbes*. I suddenly felt a panic set in, as though I was going on a blind date, and I began to worry that I didn't deserve a second of her time. The first person that came in the room was Henry, her business partner. Later I would find out he was not just her right-hand man, but her longtime friend. We were in the middle of casual chit-chat, getting to know each other, when Michelle walked in.

My eyes grew wide. Right in front of me was Michelle Phan, in the flesh. I suddenly didn't know what to say, and my eyes darted around not knowing if I should look at her or not. Even from the corner of my eye, I could see she was exactly as I had expected.

"Hi! I'm Michelle! I heard a lot about you guys from Jennifer!" She said it bright and cheerily. I remember she had friendly eyes, and her voice was as smooth and buttery as ever.

"Hi, I'm Charlotte, and this is Dave," I said as coolly as possible. Dave and I both shook her hand in a professional fashion.

"I'm a huge fan," I then blurted out. Very smooth, Charlotte, I thought to myself. She didn't know this at the time, but three years before, I had stood in line at the Kimpton Eventi Hotel in New York with a long line of young fans and their moms. She was launching a new palette collection for EM, and I wanted to thank her for always talking about Korean beauty on her channel. Her constant praise had made her fans seek it out, and Soko Glam had benefited. I stood in line for over an hour for a chance to meet Michelle and take a photo. Luckily I was able to hand off a bag of products to her and hoped she would read my personal note (there wasn't time to say much due to the rushed meet and greet).

As we sat down, we started to talk. I shared how we had started Soko Glam and what our plans were for the future. It felt wonderful to connect with a fellow Asian-American in the space, considering the beauty industry was largely dominated by Caucasian men and women. There weren't many people who looked like me having the same experiences. I remember feeling thankful that Jennifer introduced us.

Michelle was quick to jump to a deep place. She told us her story matter-of-factly. For over 10 years, her role in the spotlight as a creator had given her opportunities that allowed her to financially care for herself and her family, something she had always dreamed of accomplishing. But with that success, she also took a hit on her happiness. She began to feel isolated, surrounded by those who saw her as a product and not as a person. Michelle felt the pressures of always selling and being in the spotlight, and insecurities and depression followed. "I wasn't in the best place, so I had to take a break," she revealed candidly. In that conference room, she shared her frustrations, her dashed dreams, and the work it took to rebuild herself mentally and professionally. (A year later, she would transparently detail this out in an emotional YouTube video titled "Why I Left.")

As she spoke, I stared at her, somewhat in disbelief. For someone who had been on the cover of *Forbes*, she was being shockingly forthcoming—and with someone she had only just met. She treated me like we knew each other well, trusting me with intimate information about her rollercoaster ride. That instantly made me feel at ease.

Her willingness to share melted away a lot of the awkwardness and made me genuinely want to help and to encourage her. It also compelled me to share that I was going through similar challenges and that she wasn't alone. As I began to open up, I realized her candid nature and desire to show not only the glamour of her life, but the stress and anxieties had encouraged me to reveal my full self too.

As Soko Glam blossomed, I was fortunate enough to meet and befriend more people who were involved in beauty and even entertainment, some of whom had millions of followers. And through these meetings, albeit sometimes brief, I began to see a pattern. I was far more impressed by and felt connected to someone who was upfront, forward, and even self-deprecating than someone who took themselves too seriously. I understand that when you have countless adoring fans, it's easy to fall into that trap. But I found a more powerful connection with people who were willing to be vulnerable.

Through the years, I was able to connect with people

like Michelle easily, even when we lived far away from each other and weren't able to meet often. The conversations we had, which were less superficial, enabled us to go deeper. I shared with her my struggles as a founder, openly and honestly. She reciprocated with her experiences and provided encouraging but firm advice, and through it all, I'm glad that we not only have jeong, but have been building that connection with every year that passes.

Those Little Sparks of Jeong

In my quest to learn more about jeong, I once asked a Korean couple in Seoul, who had just been married for six months, if they had jeong with each other. To my surprise, they explained that even though they had committed to each other for the rest of their lives through marriage, they were still in the process of developing jeong. I began to understand that jeong shouldn't be taken for granted, given the sheer amount of effort involved. If newlyweds were in the process of building jeong, it was obviously something that took a great deal of time.

But don't let that discourage you. Even the initial sparks of jeong that occur—even with strangers!—can make a lasting impression. And though every relationship will not reach its fullest point, there is a great deal of value in living by the principles of jeong. If you show your authentic self and give without expecting anything in return; if you spend quality time with the people you care about, your life will feel more rewarding, whether jeong develops or not. At the end of the day, I've found that leading with the intent of building jeong makes a huge impact in your life—it certainly has in mine.

My colleagues at Soko Glam and Then I Met You, both past and present, know this well too. We've been through a lot together, and I have seen with my own two eyes the amount of hard work and creativity that they have poured into all that they do to ensure every product, every campaign, and every experience is the best of its class. Sometimes we have the literal sweat taken out of us. In the summer of 2019, we created our first long-term retail experience called Soko House, which would stand for two months as an enormous shop and skin care experience in Soho. We had never done anything like it. Physically, we were moving boxes the entire weekend before, then we were all working evenings and weekends to create something special for our community that summer. The warm feelings we received from our customers in turn made everything worth it, and all the sweat we shed brought us closer together.

I've seen my colleagues support and rally together, and I've seen lifelong friendships form from these experiences. Our team has gone through many challenges together, which can bring about jeong—sometimes *goweon*, other times *miweon*. Though many of our teammates have come and gone, our shared experiences will always tie us together, like an invisible string, and I will always be thankful.

The last spark of jeong I'd like to share took place in Poland in 2017, where I've been lucky to have supportive fans from day one. I was fortunate enough to be invited to the country for a second round of book signing events for *The Little Book of Skin Care*, which I published in 2015. The morning of the signing, I remember feeling shocked by the long line waiting for me at Douglas, a leading European beauty retailer. I learned that people had traveled so far—some for several hours by train—just to see me. Due to the length of the line, I was told to keep things moving by limiting my interactions to just signing the book with no small talk. I ignored the event agency's request and spent a few minutes asking each person questions, getting to know them, answering any skin care questions they had, and to write personalized notes after I got to know their interests. I took multiple photos, until each person was satisfied. I knew that despite my limited time, I wanted to ensure my fans had a good experience getting to talk to me and see me instead of something that was generic and too short-lived.

Even though it's impossible to have deeply rooted jeong with every single fan, it was a small way to show my gratitude and go just a little bit deeper. My hope was that the small spark of jeong between us could last a few extra minutes and create a memory that could last a lifetime.

Simple Acts of Jeong

- *The next time* you catch up with a friend on the phone, through video chat, or in person, don't be afraid to put down your guard. Instead of the standard "how are you, I'm good!" share one positive in your life and one challenge that you are struggling with. This can set the stage for a more genuine conversation and avoid the pitfalls of superficial chats.

- *With that said*, make sure you are being an honest friend in return. Be truthful and firm when you need to be and don't sugarcoat. Truthful conversations create real responsibility—what's shared in confidence should never be shared with others. Gossip is not only hurtful and divisive, it's unfair to the friend who put their full self on the line to confide in you. Trust is key!

- *Remember that when your friend is speaking*, it is your time to listen and hear them out without judgment. Fewer words are often better—you don't always have to analyze the situation and give your advice or overtake the conversation by sharing your personal experiences. A good rule of thumb: Before you jump in and start responding, ask yourself honestly why you're talking. Are you free of judgement? Do you have an agenda? Be self-aware of what you're about to say to ensure you're not chiming in for other reasons, i.e. finding a way to inject your experiences as a way to humblebrag. Share your honest thoughts, but also be thoughtful about what you say. With jeong, it's less about what you say, but how you make them feel.

Chapter 7

Not Me, But We

I WAS NOT ALWAYS A SKIN CARE EXPERT. BEFORE MY time in Korea, before I had been professionally trained as an esthetician, I didn't have experience in traditional beauty industry roles like sales, marketing, or product development. In fact, I barely knew the difference between a toner and an exfoliator, and I was skeptical either had any effect. What I liked, though, was that the world of skin care felt like a secret club without any admission criteria. I was instantly ushered in with open arms by my friends in Korea. We would share skin tips over lunch at the office, or ooh and ahh over each other's *ssang ul* (bare-faced looks) at brunch on the weekends, chatting about what products we'd been using. Our group mentality encouraged exploration and was highly engaging since we had a crew that shared advice and cheered each other along the way. I found something particularly inclusive and universal about the beauty space, and I felt this no matter who I was speaking to. The sentiment carried over even when I moved back to the U.S., coming through in my countless conversations with fellow skin care lovers, from Then I Met You customers to beauty influencers and editors.

Here's more proof that the skin care experience is communal. Take a quick peek at the products in your cabinet and consider when and where you were motivated to buy each one. Chances are you found most of them by word-of-mouth, either through friends or through a post on social media from someone skin-savvy that wanted to share all the benefits in great detail. Think about the last time *you* found a holy grail beauty product, like a cleansing balm with a texture just like sorbet or a gentle chemical exfoliant that made your skin feel sparkly smooth and poreless. It's natural that you'd want to sing its praises from the mountaintops for everyone to hear. You'd swear about the amazing effects to the friends around you, and if you're a thorough person (like me!), you'd provide before and after photos as proof. (For this reason, I find beauty to be different from the fashion experience. Not only is style particular to a certain taste, if you find an incredible new boutique or designer, it's not always in your best interest to spread the word. Imagine showing up to an event to find someone wearing the exact same outfit as you—a cringe-inducing moment that I wouldn't wish on anyone.)

I've seen the communal vibes of skin care play out over and over again. When we opened Soko House, I remember watching two friends walk in that first day. One woman, who I knew was a devout Soko Glam customer, without hesitation grabbed a basket and started throwing in cleansers, pimple patches, and sheet masks. At the same time, she started coaching her friend, telling her about all her favorites and the nuances behind each skin care step. Another time, I saw a pair of strangers standing in line at an event in Nolita for Then I Met You's pop-up. Once they'd reached the front, they told me they'd become fast friends by bonding over the fact that The Cleansing Duo had helped them both curb their hormonal acne. Later that year, the pair arrived together at another one of our events and shared with me how they now held each other accountable with their routines.

I've been a part of and even hosted skin care gatherings in more intimate settings, sometimes in the comfort of someone's own home. It always felt perfectly natural to talk about our most trusted products and tips over glasses of wine. The same sense of community persists online too.

Just take a look at the reviews on Soko Glam's site. There are hundreds of them, sometimes paragraphs long, obviously written with care to help others who might have a similar skin type or skin goals. Of course this goes for positive and negative experiences; if a product is not suited for you, you'd take the time to write a cautionary tale. Either way, I love this communal sensibility and consider it essential to what we do. We make it a point to never delete or hide reviews, and we never take part in review programs that send free products to influencers in exchange for coverage, in case they aren't in it for the right reasons. I want to nurture the community and the trust within it.

My point is that the relationship-driven nature of skin care reminded me so much of the bonds formed through jeong. From my days in Seoul to my time with Soko Glam and Then I Met You, it was always the same. When your skin improved, everyone was elated for you. If you had a recurring issue, everyone would jump in to support and provide guidance, without expecting anything in return. After all, skin care is a journey, and we navigate it together without fear of showing our full selves, in our bare-faced glory.

Simple Acts of Jeong

Make Time for Self-Care

Although I've mainly described jeong as the deep connection you have with *others*, like your best friends or family members, I believe jeong can be interpreted to reflect on the relationship you have with yourself, as well.

These days, we are inundated with commitments and bombarded with technology; to be "busy" is somewhat considered a virtue in this era of non-stop hustling. But as you're instructed to secure yourself before you assist others on an airplane, the same logic applies here. If you're unable to take care of your mental health foremost, there's no way you'll be in the right frame of mind to forge bonds with others.

Investing in a skin care routine allows you to pamper yourself, giving you time to reflect and unwind every morning and night. It can be as simple as a four-step routine that gets your skin pampered with the essentials, or as long and lengthy as a 30-minute session with rose-infused exfoliating masks. Whatever you choose, it will both energize you for the day and keep you relaxed throughout the evenings (As a new mother, this has been crucial for my mental health!).

When I created Then I Met You, I personally wanted to infuse the ethos of jeong, so that whenever you hear or see its name, you'll think of someone or something that changed your life for the better—a memory that is intimate and personal to you. As Then I Met You sits on your vanity, my hope is that whenever you look at it, you'll be reminded of this philosophy and the life-changing magic of cultivating jeong.

Meditation is another incredible tool for self-care, and apps like Headspace make it incredibly easy to carve out 10–15 minutes of your day to put your mind at ease and be more aware and in control of the millions of thoughts that come racing through your mind. I had my share of misconceptions about the process (it sounded both tedious and time-consuming), until Dave asked me to meditate with him in the mornings. Now it's become a part of our daily routine: After we walk Rambo, we take 10 minutes to meditate. It was easier to begin with a partner and a set time to do it. As a result, I've felt more focused and at ease throughout the day.

A Closer Look at Collectivism

So now you know that it was the community aspect of skin care that drew me in. And it was that same focus on community over self that also made me a believer in jeong. Jeong is built around collectivism, the practice of giving priority to the group rather than any individual in the group. To understand why jeong stems from this mindset, I want to share a little of the history of jeong that helped me understand its importance.

Mr. Hong once told me that jeong became an important part of our culture due to the long history of Koreans working in villages, mainly as farmers. A devastating flood or a drought one year could quickly lead to widespread famines and other hardships, so it was imperative that the entire village work together for their survival. Typically, the villagers would pitch in and share field work and resources for the harvest, and then split the gains equally.

In these villages, there was even a way to get a loan from your community called *gye*. In lieu of a traditional bank loan, a *gye* allowed lump sums to be consolidated among trusted members of the community then distributed to any of those members at strategic times of need.

This money was helpful for various matters, whether to buy land, support a child, or help a sick family member. Believe it or not, the practice of *gye* still happens today. I remember when I was a child, my parents participated in a monthly *gye* with a group of fellow Korean liquor store owners in Los Angeles. As fresh immigrants with little to no credit, it was difficult for them to receive financial assistance from the bank. So every month, the members would contribute money to a collective "pot," and that same month, one person in the group would take the total home to spend on their own business or personal needs.

When it was my parents' turn to benefit from *gye*, I distinctly remember how helpful it was, as they used it to expand the store. My dad bought new equipment, like a fridge and a water filtration system to offer a bottled water service to his customers. He told me that without the deep connection that existed between the members of the group, *gye* would not be possible, as it was primarily based on your word and not a written contract. We'd heard of cases where people would run away with the money; other times, if a family had fallen on hard times, they could no longer contribute to the fund—it wasn't a foolproof plan, but it was one based on trust and shared goodwill. *Gye* was about the benefit of the collective. Even though you had to wait patiently for your turn to reap the benefits, you still participated every month to support the growth of everyone in the group.

Woori Is We

In the Korean language, the word *woori* (we or our) has great importance due to the nature of jeong. For example, people regularly say *woori nara* (our nation) rather than "my nation" or even *woori eomeoni* (our mother), which is often used to reference someone as a maternal figure, even if technically the woman is not the speaker's biological mother. This usage is a nod to the collectivist attitude of the nation.

Another example of this mindset can be found in Korean wedding and mourning traditions. Both weddings and funerals are widely attended, not only by close friends and family, but members of your wider network, and they always involve a form of monetary support. You receive wedding invites *left* and *right* from people you hardly know, and though you're not obligated to attend unless you are close, you would still be expected to send a contribution. Even though my wedding to Dave took place in the U.S., the whole department still gave me wedding money. One VP even called me into his office and gave me 1,000,000 Korean won (about $1,000 USD), all in cash, stuffed in a long white envelope. I was shocked by this unexpected generosity, and I remember walking out of his office in a daze.

Funerals function in the same way. I remember any time that a colleague at Samsung had a family member pass away—anyone within their family, from grandparents to aunts and uncles to second cousins—every member on the team would automatically contribute money to help with funeral expenses. Sometimes the company itself would even contribute a standing wreath at the funeral hall to pay their respects.

Whenever possible, us team members would go together to the funeral home to also pay respects (the company would always share when someone's family member had passed away, along with the funeral date and location, on an official message board). First we would turn in our cash envelope to the person collecting. Then we would perform a deep bow before a portrait of the deceased in a special room. Afterward, we would eat a simple meal provided by the family alongside other people paying their respects in a cafeteria-like setting, with a bottle of soju on each table. I always found this special: Even if it was someone you had never known, we would still come together to show our support for our colleague in their time of sorrow, as they would do for ours.

Many historians also point to the centuries of colonization by Japan and China as one contributing factor toward Korea's collectivist mentality. Koreans had to rise up together to fight for their independence, and many willingly sacrificed their lives for the cause, which could not have happened if they did not share deep jeong for their nation and for their people as a whole. While war stories featuring patriotic heroes and heroines are not unique to Korea, the fact remains that this large part of the country's history impacted its society and paved the way for a culture that works more toward the benefit of the greater good.

As a millennial that has lived in the U.S. for most of my life, I grew up in a society that rewards individualism.

Our constitution and its civil liberties are focused on the individual and their pursuit of happiness. Layer on the fact that capitalism is the very foundation that the country was built upon, and individualism seems to have only grown stronger with time. As a result, I believe I've been conditioned to have a "me me me" mentality, where I focus on myself first and foremost, before anyone else.

But feeling jeong made me think a little harder. It was the thought of my parents no longer having to spend late nights standing in front of a register that became the wind on my back when I needed to burn the midnight oil. It was the camaraderie of my colleagues and the thought of taking part in something bigger than myself that made me want to make the right choices. My heart felt full of warmth and gratitude when I spent the long holiday weekend of *Chuseok* with my uncle, aunt, and cousins. We would play traditional folk games like *yut-nori* on their living room floor, tossing up wooden sticks and shuffling pennies across a simple diagram etched out on white paper in pen to mark our place. With jeong comes loyalty, commitment, trust, and respect.

That's why learning about jeong in Korea inspired me to lead a life that focuses on thinking about others first.

Seeing it work in my personal and professional life sparked something in me. Although I do need constant reminders because it's not entirely my natural inclination, I believe that consciously thinking about the community—not just myself—will help me live a meaningful life.

Understanding Han Through Korean Cinema

Korean films often cover the history of colonization, and many of them make me weep without fail (Korean cinema and dramas have really nailed how to express jeong!). My top three movies set in this era: *Assassination* starring Jeon Ji-Hyun, *Last Princess* starring Son Ye-Jin, and *My Way* starring Jang Dong-Gun. If you're looking for more historical context and you're in Korea, visit the Seodaemun Prison museum, the site where Koreans who resisted the Japanese occupation were held.

With *Han*, Comes Jeong

It's finally time to talk about *han*, which I first mentioned all the way back in Chapter 2. The word is used to describe a sorrow and even a bitterness and regret that developed among Korean people as the country endured more than 20 centuries of oppression, war, and famine. Some historians say those shared experiences and collective sadness altered the very essence of Korean character. Even though the country is no longer in a state of active war or under colonialist rule, it is said that the pain felt by the previous generations was so deep that it remains present in Korean people today. It was in the 20th century that *han* was popularized in public discourse as a specifically Korean characteristic.

The folk song "Arirang," widely considered one of Korea's national anthems, originated in the early 20th century as a song of resistance during Japanese colonial rule. When I listen to it, I can understand why people of all ages feel that it expresses both the melancholy grief and passionate energy of the Korean spirit.

Not Me, But We

An English Translation of "Arirang"

> *Arirang, Arirang, Arariyo...*
> *You are going over Arirang Hill.*
>
> *My love, you are leaving me*
> *Your feet will be sore before you go 10 li* [4 km].
>
> *Just as there are many stars in the clear sky,*
> *There are also many dreams in our heart.*

Han is as much a part of Korean culture as jeong, and I am calling attention to it because of their strong correlation. It is said that jeong is often born out of *han*. While Koreans have felt the long-lasting effects of regret and sorrow (*han*), they have also responded by creating tight bonds (jeong), working together to make sacrifices for the good of the collective. For example, during the IMF Crisis (also known as the Asian Financial Crisis) in 1988, families donated their gold jewelry to help the country out of its economic crisis. Again, these were everyday normal Korean families donating their personal treasures to the government to melt down and sell in the international markets.

Currently, our generation is dealing with a traumatic time of our own on an unprecedented global scale. The Covid-19 pandemic of 2020 has resulted in hundreds of thousands of deaths in the U.S. alone; there are many who are suffering from health complications, even months after recovery. As the number of cases continue to soar, the negative impact on everything, from small businesses to education, has been devastating for people around the world. Our normal way of life has been completely disrupted, and we are constantly filled with anxiety and despair for our health and the health of our loved ones. Perhaps the most mentally draining fact is that we don't know when the pandemic will end, nor do we currently know the extent of the lasting damage to our society. This accumulated feeling of despair and regret that we are experiencing due to the pandemic reminds me of the heartache of Korean *han*, which continues to grow as time goes on.

In a sense, as we live through this pandemic, we will experience our own *han*, a dark cloud of complex emotions. Yet from bitterness and feelings of woe and anguish, we can also find a tinge of hope for the future. Although we as humans have been brought down by a disease we are still trying to understand, jeong has become like a shield that keeps us protected by camaraderie and support. I have seen simple acts of jeong in action in the middle of a pandemic. In New York, I've seen hotels and businesses offering room, board, and other essentials to medical staff to ensure they are quarantined away from family members; I've also seen medical workers selflessly flying out to hospitals that are short-staffed in hard-hit epicenters of the pandemic. Together, we shelter under this umbrella of jeong, and it gives us strength.

Beyond the pandemic, there are countless tragedies that occur day by day. They seem endless, and we don't know when or where they will strike. As we go through life navigating our own challenges, I hold onto the belief that jeong with others can offer us much needed comfort and offer something good and inspiring out of even the hardest and darkest of times.

Why Empathy Is the Way Forward

Fortunately, I don't think you *have* to have *han* to experience jeong. The main takeaway is that empathy opens the door to jeong. The ability to understand and share another person's experiences as if they are your own is crucial. If you're unable to truly understand what another person is going through, it will be hard for you to connect on a meaningful level.

Here's a simple, personal example of how empathy can give you perspective and create deeper bonds with others. When I first began curating for Soko Glam, my personal skin concerns had always been my dull, dry complexion and the visible pores along my nose. I didn't have sensitive skin, nor did I deal with acne at the time, so in the grand scheme of things, I was blessed with a relatively clear complexion. Naturally, this meant I focused more on curating products for dry skin types like myself that wanted a hydrated glow.

Then one day, I received a heartfelt email from a follower about how her acne had affected her self-esteem and her social life, to the point where she didn't want to go to school or even outside of her home. I felt she was crying out for help. At that point, I had never experienced anything close to what she had, but the letter left me in tears. How sad and alone she must have felt, to the extent that she didn't even want to leave her house. Empathy gave me perspective and moved me to jump into action and curate more products for those struggling with acne-prone skin (Little did I know that when I hit 30 a few years later, I would have my own persistent bout of hormonal acne and would truly feel how crushing and aggravating it could be).

But you don't have to go through the same challenges as someone else to become empathetic. Empathy can actually be learned and developed, and if you take the time to hone and practice this soft skill, it can make you a better friend, family member, spouse, teacher, and even a better boss. Even taking intentional effort to be present, observe their body language, ask thoughtful questions, or imagine yourself in their shoes are ways to practice empathy, and could be the way you carve a path toward a jeong-filled relationship. Andy Puddicombe, a former Buddhist monk and the cofounder of Headspace, said it best on the company's website: "Empathy does not require that we have been through the same thing as another person, simply that we meet them where they are now."

As we attempt to solve some of our world's most deeply rooted problems—a global pandemic, income disparity, and systemic social injustices (a few top of mind at the moment)—I often wonder if we're in this predicament in the first place because we've slowly lost our ability to be empathetic. It makes me think about how different our world would be if we were able to master this mindset and skill. My hunch is that more empathy would lead to more jeong, and through those shared and meaningful connections, people would feel more understood, respected, and valued. To me, a world with more empathy feels like a better life worth living.

How to Practice Empathy to Build Jeong

It takes practice and education to develop real empathy—to truly feel what another person is feeling or experiencing. Here are a few more ways to hone your empathy skills and use them as a pathway to build jeong with others.

1. Quality vs. Quantity

Social media apps and email allow us to connect with many more people, but that often means more quantity in interactions over quality. It also means we're more inclined to make assumptions about people we don't know, based on what they share online. Instead of jumping to conclusions, take the time to meet people in real life, especially those who you would not normally talk to or spend time with. Instead of small talk (i.e. the weather and work), ask questions about their beliefs and their daily lives. Consider how their routine is different from yours and why. Instead of challenging them, try to listen to their opinions without judgment.

2. Don't Downplay Their Pain

When a person is struggling, they will be comforted by your empathy, not your sympathy. Note that empathy and sympathy have two different meanings: Sympathy is feeling sorry for an individual, which means you are pitying their circumstance. Too often we provide sympathy because we don't know how to react.

Try not to fall into the common trap of attempting to cheer someone up by talking about something positive. I'm guilty of saying things like, "It could be worse . . ." or "At least you're feeling healthy . . ." (when someone they love is sick). This is not what people want to hear when they are confiding in you with their struggles. Essentially, you are diminishing or disregarding their pain.

Instead, acknowledge their suffering with statements like, "I'm sorry you're going through this," or, "I'm here for you, let me know how I can help." Sometimes a hug is all that they need. Whenever I am feeling stressed or overwhelmed, my sister Michelle's presence alone makes me feel comforted and secure (although the warm, home-cooked meals she makes when I visit do help). For a concrete action (given any socially distanced constraints), consider sending someone a card or a dish they like to eat. Empathy doesn't have to cost you, though; you can call to check in and be the person who listens patiently, no matter what grievances they need to air. Remember, it's about them and not you. Every gesture counts.

Chapter 8

In the Mood for Jeong

WHENEVER I WAS FEELING PARTICULARLY LONELY in Seoul, I would simply ride the light blue subway line one hour north from Yeoksam Station to Miasamgeori (now known as Miasageori Station), a 10-minute walk from my aunt and uncle's house. One of my cousins, Minyoung *unnie*, still lived with her parents since she was unmarried at the time. We were similar in age and she spoke English well, so we became close and I naturally became a frequent visitor. It was always a welcome reprieve from the stress of office work or the pressure to have the latest designer bag being carried by all the well-heeled women in the city. Their home was a place I could just be myself, surrounded by those who simply wanted the best for me and cocooned by the jeong that we shared.

As much as I connected with Minyoung *unnie*, her dad, who was in his 70s, truly made my visits special. Despite his age, my uncle was boisterous and filled with a charismatic energy that could always be felt in any room. He had a knack for making the little things feel grand, like when he would surprise us with a bag full of red bean ice cream bars from the convenience store. Without meaning to, he led by example: As soon as the weather got colder, I reciprocated by surprising everyone with *bungeoppang*, warm red bean stuffed into a crispy fish-shaped pastry that was sold at the street food carts near the subway stairs. By witnessing his generosity and seeing how much impact a simple surprise could make, I had understood how it felt even better to give, without expecting anything in return.

Each time I came over, I loved hearing him speak. Even though we had grown up in completely different generations, we were always on the same page. On days we would watch TV together, I would deliberately flip to the news channel, so that I could listen attentively to his perspective on life and politics. He held such strong convictions, and I found myself respecting his wisdom. It compelled me to ask more questions about the protests, or the state of the economy and his satisfaction with the current Korean president—things I didn't even think to ask my own parents.

I often think about how he was and still remains the glue that made his family such a strong unit. He was stern when needed, but generous with his compliments. Despite having some trouble and pain while walking, he hardly looked a day older than 60, thanks to the jet black hair that he took care to dye every month. His smooth skin and prominent, chiseled jawline remained from his youth. He spent his whole life working as a taxi driver to support his family of five and was proud of his ability to provide for them, not only financially, but emotionally. He held such a tender, soft spot for his three daughters and his grandchildren, and it was clear that he took great joy in his role as a husband, father, and grandfather. I will always be thankful that he and my aunt extended those same feelings to me during my time in Korea.

Though he lived a modest life, he was the most generous person I knew. And after a full day spending time on the couch with him and his family, I always pondered on the subway ride home why my heart felt so full. In many ways, they were the ones who taught me about jeong and the importance of developing deep bonds with each other. Through my time with them, I understood that having jeong with others was proof of true wealth in your life.

Time With Family and Friends
Heals the Soul

Most often, you will have the greatest jeong with family members and childhood friends. They are the people that will call you out when you've done something silly or when you have something stuck in your teeth. They'll make fun of your dancing. You can be at your absolute worst, but they will still stick by your side. Jeong with your closest inner circle is cultivated through trials and triumphs. It takes time to build these relationships, but these are the people that will have your back forever.

Treasure these relationships and nurture them. Show and share your appreciation, constantly, through words and actions. Call them out of the blue to tell them you miss them or just how much they mean to you. Celebrate them and make them feel special by taking the time to visit them, preparing a special meal, or planning an outing. Make them a priority, even over work. If you have a falling out, consider making amends by taking the first step toward forgiveness. It's not always easy, but once you have jeong with someone, that's all the more reason to put differences aside and give your best effort to salvage that rare relationship.

I know we tend to get caught up in our own lives (out-of-sight, out-of-mind). Even I let years slip away, prioritizing work above everything else. But at the end of the day, you only have a finite amount of time on this earth, and you should treasure your loved ones. When needed, bend over backward to support them and love them. You'll be thankful when they reciprocate when you need it the most.

Luck or Jeong?

Once I moved to New York, I wasn't able to see them as often, but on one of my many trips back to Korea for business, I took the time to visit my aunt at a local hospital. She was there to undergo a long-awaited surgery to take care of the pain she had in her right leg. Armed with some red ginseng extract for tea (my go-to gift for any Koreans around my parents' age), I navigated my way to the hospital, which was in a fairly remote part of Seoul I had not been to before. When I finally arrived and went up to her room, I remember how shocking it was to suddenly see my aunt on a hospital bed. Suddenly, I became emotional. Trying to hold back my tears before she could notice, I averted my gaze toward the other women who were sharing her room. There were at least five other occupied beds, some surrounded by family members snacking on peeled tangerines. I felt better seeing that no one seemed to be in pain. They were all fairly preoccupied with a reality TV show playing on a small 14-inch set that sat squarely on top of a mini fridge in the center of the room. Fortunately, my aunt was her usual chatty self, scolding me for "wasting" my money on tea, and all seemed right with the world.

After visiting hours were over, my uncle and I decided to have a late dinner together at a restaurant in a small alleyway by the hospital that was known for its lamb skewers. We caught up, chatting about my parents and siblings over the Tetris-like array of side dishes, the piping hot soup, and the rotating skewers. He asked how Dave was doing and why he hadn't made it out to Korea this time. I explained that things were too chaotic in New York for him to join me. Although I had never filled my uncle in on all the details, he had heard through the grapevine about how large Soko Glam had grown. I'm sure some of the updates had come from snippets of conversations with my dad, but my uncle apparently read about the company directly on Naver after several media outlets had covered the rise of Korean beauty in the U.S. and Soko Glam's prominent role as the leading player. Without me having to say much, he knew things were going well.

"Charlotte, you know, you have a lot of *bok*," he said knowingly in Korean, as he turned the skewers and handed me the first well-done piece. He had said this to me before, years ago, when I had first gotten the opportunity to work at Samsung in 2008. He too had been surprised that I somehow bypassed all the rigorous testing and assessments typically required of people joining the company.

As I accepted the skewer with two hands and began nibbling on it, I began to turn that word around in my head. *Bok* was the Korean word for luck. I distinctly knew this word because at the turn of every calendar year, before everyone took off for the holidays, everyone would greet each other with the phrase, "새해 복 많이 받으세요," (sae-hae bok mani badeuseyo) which meant, "wishing you a lot of luck in the New Year." And then when Lunar New Year rolled around again roughly two months later, we would say it once more.

My natural reaction had always been to nod agreeably with whatever my uncle said, but I stopped myself. Though I understood where he was coming from, on this rare occasion, I actually disagreed with him. For most of my life I too had chalked up all my fortunes and happiness to luck. That had been the easiest explanation. There had been times when I had felt so lucky that I had stared at the ceiling wide awake at night, wondering if I had been given *too* much. In my mind, I was an ordinary girl who was not spectacular at anything in particular, yet I was living in extraordinary circumstances. Sometimes paranoia would get the best of me, and I'd wonder if there was something horrible waiting for me—lurking behind some ominous corner because I had already used up all the luck that one could have in a lifetime.

But I felt at odds with my uncle's words that day because I had gained a completely new perspective that I still maintain. Luck relies on the idea that success or failure is up to chance, rather than a result of one's actions. It is this elusiveness of luck—something that is completely out of one's control—that I disagree with. My firm belief is that my happiness and my personal fulfillment are not a product of luck. It is all due to jeong.

Jeong Leads to Success and Happiness

There were several pivotal moments in my life that led me to where I am today. Looking back now, I can see that each one of them was in fact an encounter with jeong. The first turning point came when I sat across those three VPs on that fateful day in Houston and was given a chance by one of the largest companies in the world. I didn't have a stacked résumé or especially impressive qualifications. I was practically fresh out of college without the bilingual skills (or any corporate skills, for that matter) that my future team would require. What had made me stand out as a candidate was my inadvertent expression of jeong for my family; it had been jeong for my grandma that had driven me to apply in the first place. And I was given that chance because one decision-maker led with jeong and decided to think with his heart, not with his head. As a result, I was rewarded with a one-way ticket to live in the city of my dreams.

The chances of me surviving in Korea's corporate world were slim. Next to nil. I was destined to drown in the unavoidable hierarchy of being a salarywoman in Korea, without the ability to communicate in the native tongue. But I didn't, thanks to the overwhelming jeong displayed by my colleagues. I was taken under their wing, and they nourished me emotionally and physically through food and their *Simple Acts of Jeong*. It was going deeper with my friends and colleagues that opened my heart to cultivate jeong for the culture, Korea, and the people as a whole. It made my loyalty and jeong unshakable, and I ended up spending the best years of my life there.

If I had not witnessed for myself the display of jeong that ordinary Koreans had for their country—when we watched the World Cup matches, or saw the dedication and self-sacrifice of Kim Yuna at the Olympics—I would have not known how far a passion for my Korean heritage could take me. Nor would I have led my life with the clear, distinct purpose of staying connected to Korea. It gave me the strength to pursue something that wasn't purely for my own selfish reasons. I wanted to walk toward a goal and a mission with a greater purpose in mind.

I have absolutely no doubt that Soko Glam wouldn't have started on the right foot without the jeong I had cultivated with my mentor Mr. Hong, or with the many friends and colleagues who would help and support me on this path. There were so many who chose to give to me without expecting anything in return. Most often they gave up their precious, unreturnable time. From a warm introduction to advice over coffee to a moment of vulnerability, there have been so many simple acts of jeong that I cannot list them all. Then, of course, there's Dave: I wouldn't have been able to build a strong foundation without him as my partner. Together we've navigated the ebbs and flows of our relationship, our business, our marriage, and now parenthood—11 years after we first met, we have welcomed our first daughter.

If I had not been able to let my guard down and be vulnerable with others, whether it was to ask for help or to simply be myself, I would never have found the genuine people I can lean on whenever I need them. I would not have been able to build the bonds and relationships with the people who I credit with keeping me grounded and for building me up. Pursuing jeong with others has taught me the importance of having empathy. Although our world is often designed to be more superficial, selfish, and less about the collective good, I have realized the importance of focusing on the "we" in our communities and of practicing empathy by pursuing quality conversations.

As you can see, jeong has reverberated through my life in mysterious ways: It opened doors and gave me a support system and the internal fortitude to pursue opportunities that I would have never imagined or thought possible for myself. I cannot deny that the results of pursuing jeong with others have made me feel more fulfilled and content, and in turn, have even made my professional life more exciting and enjoyable.

Why We Need Jeong Now—More Than Ever

I feel a deeper sense of urgency to spread this message now due to the common belief that there has been a gradual decline of jeong, even in Korea. It's something that has been happening for a while, as I've heard from native Koreans and noticed myself on recent visits. Some attribute this to the rise of capitalism due to the country's economic success in the past few decades, as well as diminishing Confucian beliefs and the technology boom, which has encouraged a more generally isolated lifestyle. This is just a small example, but nowadays when I'm on the subway in Seoul, almost everyone I see is staring at their smartphones, wrapped up in their messaging apps, watching videos, or playing games. They simply forget what it means to be present and value what makes us a collective species. This is not unique to Seoul, but applies to the world we live in now. Of course, due to the pandemic, this feeling of isolation and the deprioritization of relationships are accelerating at an even faster pace.

As I walked around Brooklyn last fall, feeling the strong and feisty kicks of my unborn daughter, I imagined a world where she too has the privilege of cultivating jeong with other people in her life. To start, I think of the deep and emotional relationship she will nourish with her grandma, a jeong that will hopefully know no limits. Perhaps like the characters in my favorite K-drama, *Reply 1988*, she too will find camaraderie and solace with friends in the neighborhood. I hoped her childhood relationships would develop into lifelong friendships. Those kids will be the ones that give her grief when she gets a funky haircut, but will be there to turn her tears into laughter when she stumbles and falls.

Above all else, I wished that jeong would lead her down a path of unexpected opportunities, just as it did for me. I can't wait to share the excitement when something extraordinary happens to her and to gently remind her that it's not due to sheer luck, but because she is the fortunate recipient of jeong. With time, I want her to also learn the importance of practicing *Simple Acts of Jeong* and to feel compelled to give generously, without expecting anything in return. I want her to help out a stranger by thinking with her heart and not always with her head. I know these lessons will impact so many decisions throughout her life and will bring incredible opportunities to people around her, not only those within her inner circle. I believe these qualities will ground her to this earth.

For these hopes to come true, I know that I need, just like my uncle, to lead by example. I will become her daily reminder to act with greater intention. I will be careful about the way we spend our time together, what I read and post online, and most importantly, the way I cherish my relationships with other people. Although this way of living doesn't always come naturally—it will always be a work in progress—I know that these *Simple Acts of Jeong* will make a difference to me and to anyone who commits to doing them. All of them will add up to a larger, sweeping change that alters our individual ways of thinking and that eventually changes our communities too. Jeong humanizes us. It's a daily reminder that with time being so finite, it's rarely the titles that we chase, the number of followers we have, or fancy things we own that bring us joy, but our long-lasting memories and relationships with people and places that matter most.

Knowing the impact of jeong, I felt motivated and inspired to spread this simple message through the platforms I have been privileged enough to build, sharing it through my social channels, infusing it into Then I Met You, and finally, writing this book. Now that you've learned more about jeong, I hope you will also be inspired to do *Simple Acts of Jeong* in an effort to experience the true power of meaningful relationships. I know that my daughter, her generation, and the one beyond it, will depend on it.

Addendum

Although I've written *The Little Book of Jeong*, I would never say this is the definitive book on the subject. Jeong has many facets and is interpreted slightly differently by each person, so if you have the opportunity, I encourage you to ask a Korean native for their own thoughts about jeong. Now that you know more about it, you can also engage with your own community to talk about jeong and what it means to you. Those discussions will take you a long way towards understanding it and applying it to your life.

The Little Book of Jeong:
Korean Glossary

The following Korean words and characters are listed in the order in which they appear.

Introduction

Jeong 정

A deep and emotional connection with a person, place, or thing that builds over time and through shared experiences.

Chapter 1

Jjigae 찌개

A Korean stew, often made with meat, seafood, or vegetables. The broth is typically seasoned with gochujang, doenjang or gangjang. It is often eaten as a communal dish and served piping hot.

Chapter 2

Han 한

An internalized feeling of sorrow, deep regret, and bitterness among Korean natives due to the country's long history of colonization.

Chapter 3

Samgyupsal, Samgyupsal-gui 삼겹살, 삼겹살구이

Grilled pork belly that has three fatty layers. A staple of Korean cuisine. It is often enjoyed at home or at Korean BBQ restaurants.

Gochujang 고추장

A red, fermented chili pepper paste that is savory, sweet, and spicy. It's often used in Korean cooking, particularly in stews.

Gim 김

Dried and edible seaweed that is a popular side dish in Korean cuisine.

Banchan 반찬

Small side dishes served alongside rice and the main dish.

Kimbap 김밥

Seaweed rolls made with cooked rice, assorted vegetables, and meat.

Seolleongtang 설렁탕

A hot soup made with ox bones and brisket. It is typically seasoned with salt, ground pepper, garlic, and spring onions.

Unnie 언니

Older sister, as addressed by females.

Nuna 누나
Older sister, as addressed by males.

Emo 이모
Auntie.

Ajuma 아줌마
Older woman.

Jondaemal 존댓말
A formal way of speaking.

Sajang-nim 사장님
President or CEO.

Eomeo-nim 어머님
Mother-in-law.

Daeri-nim 대리님
Assistant manager.

Yeogi-yo 여기요
The phrase used for "here" or "excuse me!"

Bibimbap 비빔밥
A large bowl of rice topped with an array of individually prepared, assorted vegetables and meat.

Poktanju 폭탄주
A "bomb shot" that is made by mixing two drinks (typically soju and beer).

Makgeolli 막걸리

A traditional Korean rice wine with 6–8 percent alcohol content.

Yakult 야쿠르트

A sweet, probiotic drink that is popular among Koreans to drink after meals.

Hweshiks 회식

Company or work dinners with colleagues that usually take place on weeknights.

Sool jip 술집

A bar or pub that serves food with the alcohol.

Anju 안주

Food made to consume with alcohol.

Haejang-guk 해장국

A variety of soups that are eaten to help ease your hangover.

Sam-cha 삼차

When bar-hopping in Korea, each place you stop is counted off as il-cha (round 1), ee-cha (round 2), sam-cha (round 3), sa-cha (round four), and so on.

Chapter 4

Sogaeting 소개팅

A blind date set up by a mutual friend.

Hanwoo beef 한우

Korea-raised cattle known for its marbling. One of the most rare and expensive types of beef.

Sa-cha 사차
Round 4 when bar-hopping (see sam-cha).

Chapter 5

Chuseok 추석
The Harvest Moon festival is a national Korean holiday, celebrated on the 15th day of the eighth lunar month of the calendar.

Chapter 7

Ssang ul 쌩얼
Bare-faced looks. A face without makeup.

Woori 우리
We or us.

Arirang 아리랑
The most famous Korean folk song, also considered the anthem of Korea.

Gye 계
A traditional way of lending capital among groups of people, without banks.

Chapter 8

Bungeoppang 붕어빵
A light fish-shaped pastry stuffed with sweetened red bean paste that is typically sold at outdoor street carts in Korea.

Bok 복
Luck

Acknowledgements

I THANK GOD FIRST AND FOREMOST, FOR NOT ONLY GIVing me the privilege to write this book, but for also giving me the experience and the wisdom to help others navigate their lives with purpose and meaning, as you have done for me.

To MK, for being an incredible editor and friend. You made this a much more enjoyable experience than I could have ever hoped. Thank you for making my words shine through in the best way possible and getting me to the finish line.

To the rest of the superstar team that made each element of the book something I can be proud of: Na Kim, Bae Sung-tae and Leah Carlson-Stanisic. And to my mentor, colleagues and friends: Mr. Hong, David Yi and Catherine Cho, who supported me emotionally with precious words of encouragement and advice.

Acknowledgments

To Dave, my rock and my best friend. Thank you for pushing me and allowing me to do what I love. You're always thinking and rooting for me, especially for my happiness. For every plate of food and fruit you prepared for me every night, for every thoughtful move you made so I could focus on writing, and for all the guidance you provided me as I wrote this book—once again you helped me achieve what I thought I could never achieve. From my personal experience, I know that Kennedy will feel supported in whatever journey she embarks on, especially with a father like you by her side.

To the teams at Soko Glam and Then I Met You, both past and present, and to my community. These stories couldn't have happened without your support and belief in me, and I will always be eternally thankful.

In many ways, this entire book has been a way to express my gratitude for all those who have been such an integral part of my journey. There are so many of you, that I cannot list them all. I hope when reading, you were able to feel the impact you've made on my life.